MORE Forgotten Stars of the 30s, 40s, and 50s

Motion Picture Stars of The Golden Age of Hollywood Who Are Virtually Unknown Today by Anyone under 50

Gary Koca

D1057741

DEDICATION

This book is dedicated to the fans of classic movies throughout the United States and the world. Also to the makers of those great films of the Golden Age of Hollywood and the stars of that era.

One explanatory note: While many of us who are fans of classic movies and the stars of that era think that these stars should not be classified as "forgotten," just mention their names to anyone under the age of 50. I am guessing that 95 percent of them have never heard of just about any of these individuals. And please remember, these are MY favorite stars who did not make it into my first book.

CONTENTS

MORE Forgotten Movie Stars of the 30s, 40s, and 50s

GARY KOCA

ACKNOWLEDGMENTS

My first book, entitled *Forgotten Movie Stars of the 30s, 40s, and 50s*, highlighted the careers of 25 stars of the Golden Era of Hollywood who were pretty big movie stars in their heyday but are virtually unknown today by almost everyone under the age of 50. They were not as well known as stars like John Wayne, Jimmy Stewart, Cary Grant, Humphrey Bogart, Bette Davis, Joan Crawford, Katharine Hepburn, or Marilyn Monroe, but were still big stars in their day.

When I did presentations on the book or talked about it, one question I often got was, "Why isn't 'so and so' in your book?" So I decided to follow that book with another effort on capturing the great stars of that era, and here it is.

I hope your favorite "so and so" is in this follow-up version.

1. ALAN LADD (1913-1964)

Officially listed at 5'6", Alan Ladd was probably a couple of inches shorter than that (Although Virginia Mayo insisted he was 5 feet 6 inches because she was 5'5" and Ladd was an inch taller than her). Nevertheless, Ladd was a major Hollywood star in the 40s and 50s. Of Alan Ladd's 100+ film and television credits over a 30+ year career, about a handful were great films and the rest mostly good or better. Of course, there was a stinker or two – he does not come across well as a sword maker turned swashbuckler in the 1964 film *The Black Knight*. Ladd's best efforts were in two film genres – westerns and film noir, and he excelled at both.

Often criticized for his acting, people who worked with him – like Mayo and Robert Preston – insisted that he was really a good actor. However, he tended to be defensive about criticism, more so even than most stars were.

Biography

Alan Walbridge Ladd was born on September 3, 1913 in Hot Springs, Arkansas, the only child of Ina Raleigh (aka Selina Rowley) and Alan Ladd, a freelance accountant. His mother was English, from County Durham, and his paternal grandparents were Canadian. Ladd never really knew his father who passed away from a heart attack when Ladd was six.At age five, he accidentally burned his apartment playing with matches, and his mother, shortly after that, moved her and her son to Oklahoma City. She married a house painter who moved them to California—think of "The Grapes of Wrath"--when he was eight because economic conditions in Oklahoma (the Dust Bowl) were bad.

As a lad, Alan picked fruit, delivered papers, and swept stores. While he was small in stature, rather shy, and not very popular, in high school he discovered track and swimming. By 1931 he was training for the 1932 Olympics, but an injury put an end to those plans. He opened a hamburger stand called Tiny's Patio (Was Ladd Tiny?), and later worked as a grip[1] at Warner Brothers Pictures. He married his friend Marjorie in 1936, but was so poor that they lived apart. In 1937, they shared a friend's apartment. They had a son, Alan Ladd Jr., and Ladd's broke, alcoholic mother moved in with them, where Ladd witnessed her suicide from ant poison a few months later. His size – extremely short for a leading man – and fair complexion were regarded as not right for movies, so he worked hard at radio, where talent scout and former actress Sue Carol – his second wife - discovered him early in 1939. After a string of bit parts in "B" pictures--and an unbilled part in Orson Welles' classic *Citizen Kane* (1941)--he tested for *This Gun for Hire* (1942) late in 1941. His fourth-billed role as psychotic killer Philip Raven made him a star. Ladd was drafted into military service in World War II in January 1943 and discharged in November with an ulcer and double hernia.

---

1 A grip in the movie business is someone who works with the camera department in setting up shots. He may also work with the electrical department in all aspects of lighting.

Throughout the 1940s his tough-guy roles packed audiences into theaters, and he was one of the very few males whose cover photos sold movie magazines. In the 1950s he was performing in lucrative but unrewarding films (an exception being what many regard as his greatest role, *Shane* (1953)). By the end of the 1950s liquor and a string of so-so films had taken their toll. In November 1962 he was found unconscious lying in a pool of blood with a bullet wound near his heart, a probable suicide attempt. In January 1964 he died at the age of 49, apparently due to a combination of alcohol and sedatives. To this day, no one is sure whether it was accidental or suicide.

So what was the reason for the immense popularity of this vertically-challenged star? A number of critics sought the explanation for Mr. Ladd's quick popularity. Bosley Crowther of The Times said, "apparently it is his tight-lipped violence that his fans love."[2]

Alan Ladd once said of himself, "I have the face of an aging choirboy and the build of an undernourished featherweight. If you can figure out my success on the screen you're a better man than I." The camera just seems to like certain movie stars, and Alan Ladd was one of them.

Awards
Alan Ladd won Golden Globe awards in 1954 and 1955 as a world film favorite. He also won Golden Apple[3] awards in 1944 and 1950 as the most cooperative actor, not surprising since he always got along extremely well with film crews.

My Favorite Alan Ladd Films
1. *Shane*
2. *This Gun for Hire*

---

2   From the New York Times' obituary on Alan Ladd.

3   The Golden Apple Award was an American award presented to entertainers by the Hollywood Women's Press Club, usually in recognition not of performance but of behavior. The award was presented from 1941 until 2001, when the Hollywood Women's Press Club became inactive. The awards ceremony included Golden Apples to recognize actors for being easy to work with.

3. *The Blue Dalia*
4. *Whispering Smith*
5. *The Badlanders*
6. *Two Years Before the Mast*

1. *Shane - (1953)*

Shane is simply one of the greatest westerns of all time, and among my favorite classic westerns.[4] *Shane* features a wonderful story, beautiful Oscar-winning photography with a setting in the hill country near Jackson Hole, Wyoming, and the Grand Tetons, with Alan Ladd as Shane dominating the film from beginning to end in a low-key, underplayed performance in which he was outstanding.

Shane (we don't even know his last name) rides into a conflict between the local cattle baron, Ryker, and a bunch of settlers, like Joe Starrett (Van Heflin) and his family, whose land Ryker wants. Joe, along with his neighbors, simply wants to build a small farm and raise his family on it. It's obvious that Shane has a background as a lawman, gunfighter, or something similar because of the way he handles himself and a gun. At first, Shane refuses to get involved, saying that he is just passing through, but when he stays with Starrett and his family, Shane realizes they are getting a raw deal from the cattleman.

On their first trip into town for supplies, Shane goes into the bar and orders a soda pop for Joe's son Joey, where he gets mocked by Ryker's men, but he does not take the bait and simply walks out; of course, Ryker and his men think Shane is simply a coward. On the next trip to town, Ryker and his men again pick on Shane, but a brawl ensues, with Shane and Joe Starrett prevailing. After this, Ryker has had enough, and he sends to Cheyenne for truly evil gunslinger Jack Wilson. You know this is going to lead to the inevitable showdown between Shane and Ryker/Wilson.

Shane is way more than simply another western about the good guys versus the bad guys. It also includes the common plot element of the old vs. new (ranchers versus farmers) and the definition of courage

4   The others are *High Noon, The Searchers, Red River, The Ox-Bow Incident,* and *My Darling Clementine.*

versus cowardice. One of the key subplots is the chemistry between Shane and Joe's wife Marian (Jean Arthur in her final movie role). Shane is obviously attracted to her, and she to him, but respects Joe Starrett too much to even consider approaching her romantically.

Directed by George Stevens, the film features a brilliant cast including Van Heflin as Joe Starrett, the aforementioned Jean Arthur as Marian, and Brandon deWilde as their son Joey. In addition, the cast includes Jack Palance as the menacingly evil Wilson, Edgar Buchanan, Emile Meyer as Ryker, Ben Johnson, and Elisha Cook, Jr., who foolishly decides he can outdraw Jack Wilson.

Shane won the Oscar for best cinematography (color) and was nominated for five other Oscars; Alan Ladd was not nominated but probably should have been. The film cost $3.1 million to make, and grossed over $20 million in the USA alone. Director George Stevens wanted Montgomery Clift and William Holden for the two leads, but they were unavailable, so he settled for Ladd and Heflin instead.

Every time I think of this film, the first thing that comes to mind is Brandon deWilde calling out "Come back, Shane" about 50 times at the end of the film as Shane moves on to his next destination.

Alan Ladd as Shane

2. *This Gun for Hire* – (1942)

Hit man Philip Raven (Alan Ladd), who's kind to children and cats, kills a blackmailer and is paid off by traitor Willard Gates (Laird

Cregar) in "hot" money. Meanwhile, pert entertainer Ellen Graham (Veronica Lake, in another film noir role), girlfriend of police Lieut. Crane (Robert Preston) is enlisted by a Senate committee to help investigate Gates. Raven, seeking Gates for revenge, meets Ellen on the train; their relationship gradually evolves from that of killer and potential victim to an uneasy alliance against a common enemy.

Alan Ladd's portrayal of the hired thug throughout the movie is surprisingly dark, even by today's standards. His character, Raven, is a man whose sole act of human compassion is not to murder a crippled orphan in cold blood, and Ladd's performance is underplayed just enough to make him chillingly believable. In fact, Ladd won a gold medal as Best Actor from *Picturegoer* magazine for his performance in this film.[5]

This Gun for Hire cost $500,000 to make and grossed over $12 million, so it was obviously very popular in 1942.

> Laird Cregar was a very good actor with a very sad ending. A very large man (6'3" and 300 pounds) he had excellent performances in films like *The Black Swan* and *I Wake up Screaming* before landing his best role as Jack the Ripper in *The Lodger*. Appearing to be older than he really was, he battled constant weight problems before dying of a heart attack at age 30.

---

5   *Picturegoer* was a popular fan magazine in the 1930s through 1950s before it merged with another fan magazine.

Laird Cregar, shown here as the detective menacing Victor Mature in the 1941 mystery *I Wake up Screaming*, with Betty Grable. Mature was 6'3" and Cregar is even taller (and heavier).

3.   *The Blue Dahlia* – 1946

Another mystery/thriller that successfully paired Alan Ladd and Veronica Lake.[6]

At the end of WWII, three buddies (Alan Ladd, William Bendix and Hugh Beaumont) return to Los Angeles where Johnny (Ladd) finds his wife in the arms of another man, Eddie (Howard Da Silva), the owner of the Blue Dahlia nightclub. When she tells Johnny that she was responsible for the death of their son because she was driving while drunk, Johnny pulls out a gun and threatens to shoot her but decides against it – she's not worth it. Later, Johnny becomes a murder suspect when his wife is found dead and Johnny becomes the prime suspect. Helped by a beautiful blonde (Veronica Lake), he tries to avoid the police while looking for the killer.

Raymond Chandler wrote the screenplay for this moody, hard-boiled film noir, which was another triumph for Ladd. He loved working with Veronica Lake because she was just under five feet tall and was a decent enough actress. By the way, Ladd and Bendix were good friends in real life, and we see Hugh Beaumont in a feature film before his days as Beaver's father in *Leave It to Beaver*.

---

6   They made a total of four films together, including *The Glass Key* (1942) - and *Saigon* (1948).

Alan Ladd and Veronica Lake, together again, in *The Blue Dahlia.*

4.   *Whispering Smith* – 1948

Whispering Smith (Alan Ladd) is a legendary iron-willed railroad detective. When his friend Murray Sinclair (Robert Preston) is fired from the railroad and begins helping Barney Rebstock, a rancher with a bad reputation, wreck trains, Smith must go after him. He also seems to have an interest in Murray's wife Marian (Brenda Marshall), and she seems to be interested in Smith also. The rest of the film involves Smith – named "Whispering" for his quiet, easygoing demeanor – attempting to round up the villains and trying to determine if Murray is on his side or not.

Alan Ladd and Robert Preston in *Whispering Smith.*

The casting of Alan Ladd and Robert Preston was a good idea. Preston tended to have a bigger-than-life personality in his films, while Ladd was always soft spoken and underplayed his parts. Plus, they were friends off screen as well. Preston always said that Ladd was a better actor than he was given credit for.[7]

You may remember Frank Faylen, the principal villain in this film – Whitey Du Sang. Faylen had a long career in movies and television, with over 200 credits. Perhaps his two most famous roles were as Dobie Gillis' dad in the television show, *The Many Loves of Dobie Gillis*, andas Ernie, the cab driver, in *It's a Wonderful Life*. Plus, he was married to actress Carol Hughes for 57 years until his death in 1985; Hughes' most notable role was as Dale Arden in the third (and worst) Flash Gordon serial, *Flash Gordon Conquers the Universe*.[8]

FrankFaylen, from *Dobie Gillis* and *It's a Wonderful life.*

5.   *The Badlanders* – 1958

---

7   *Whispering Smith* was made into a 1961 television show starring another soft-spoken actor, Audie Murphy.

8   Of course, the beautiful Jean Rogers played Dale in the first two Flash Gordon serials - *Flash Gordon* and *Flash Gordon's Trip to Mars* and was far superior to Hughes. Buster Crabbe played Flash in all three Flash Gordon serials (1936, 1938, and 1940), and also played Buck Rogers in the very mediocre serial of the same name (1939).

Two men are released from the Arizona Territorial Prison at Yuma in 1898. One, the Dutchman (Alan Ladd), is out to get both gold and revenge from the people of a small mining town who had him imprisoned unjustly. The other, McBain (Ernest Borgnine), is just trying to go straight, but that is easier said than done once the Dutchman involves him in his gold theft scheme.

McBain rescues a Mexican woman (Katy Jurado) from men who accost her on the street. After that, she, McBain, and the Dutchman become good friends. The rest of the film involves the two men in a plot to extract ore from a mine while trying to avoid being killed in the process.

Again, I really liked the pairing of the soft-spoken Ladd with the outspoken Borgnine. An unlikely combination but it worked. In this film, Borgnine met his future wife, Katy, and they were married about a year after this film was released. Jurado's fiery personality was more than a match for Borgnine, however; the marriage only lasted four years.

6.   *Two Years Before the Mast* – 1946

In real life, while an undergraduate at Harvard College, writer Richard Henry Dana had an attack of the measles which affected his vision. Thinking it might help his sight, Dana left Harvard to enlist as a common sailor on a voyage around Cape Horn on the brig *The Pilgrim*. He returned to Massachusetts two years later, aboard the *Alert* (which left California sooner than the *Pilgrim*). Dana kept a diary throughout the voyage, and, after returning, he wrote a recognized American classic, *Two Years Before the Mast*, published in 1840. The novel was made into a film in 1946.

In the film version, Charles Stewart, the "Pilgrim" owner's playboy son (Alan Ladd), finds himself shanghaied on his father's ship commanded by cruel Captain Francis Thompson (Howard Da Silva). When scurvy breaks out, attributable to unbearable conditions brought about by the captain, Stewart leads a mutiny and is slapped in irons and flogged. Richard Henry Dana is played by Brian Donlevy, who keeps a diary of his two years on the ship. The cast also includes William Bendix as the tough but respected first mate and Barry Fitzgerald as the ship's cook.

10

Probably the best member of the cast is Howard Da Silva as the captain, basically an American version of Captain Bligh. Though Alan Ladd was no Clark Gable[9], *Two Years Before the Mast* is an excellent sea adventure with a very good cast.

Howard da Silva was one of 324 actors, writers and directors who fell victim to the Hollywood blacklisting of the early 1950s, and had his career halted in the blink of an eye. My favorite Da Silva role was as Benjamin Franklin in the 1972 musical *1776!* with William Daniels as John Adams and Ken Howard as Thomas Jefferson.

Ken Howard, Howard Da Silva, and William Daniels in *1776!* Here they are celebrating the egg, in essence the birth of the new United States of America.

Soft-spoken Alan Ladd was particularly good at film noir and western roles, because he almost always underplayed his character rather than overacted. His charisma, immense popularity, and ability to humanize the gangster/hoodlum, ensured the continued development of the film noir genre of film in Hollywood. And his movies have generally held up better than he could have imagined. His last great role, *Shane*, came in what many consider to be THE American western.

---

9   Clark Gable was Fletcher Christian, the hero in *Mutiny on the Bounty*.

2. Robert Preston (1918-1987)

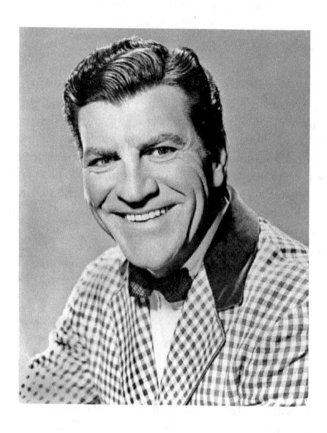

Since I started this book with Alan Ladd, why not move to a friend of his, Robert Preston? While Ladd was shy and reserved, Preston was outgoing – I don't think he was ever accused of underplaying his parts. While Preston is, of course, most well known for his role as Professor Harold Hill in *The Music Man* – a role he was born to play, both on Broadway and in the film version – he had many other notable roles in a film, television, and stage career that lasted for almost 50 years. In fact, some of his best work was performed in the 1980s although for purposes of this book, I will concentrate mainly on his earlier career in the 30s through 50s.

Robert Preston's long career in film and on stage began when he joined a traveling theater company when he was only 16. In 1938 he signed a contract with Paramount Pictures and caught the public's attention in the railroad drama *Union Pacific* with Barbara Stanwyck. But his greatest success came, of course, with his portrayal of the charismatic huckster in *The Music Man*. Preston won two Tony Awards during his career.

Biography

Actor Robert Preston Meservey was born on June 8, 1918, in Newton Highlands, Massachusetts. But his family moved, and he grew up in Los Angeles, the son of a garment worker and a record store clerk, and started his acting career as a teenager. He was also a trained musician, playing several instruments and in high school became interested in theater. Not surprisingly, at only 16 years old, Robert left school to join a traveling theater company. Shortly thereafter, he joined the Pasadena Community Playhouse[10], taking classes and appearing in scores of plays alongside such soon-to-be-well-known actors as Dana Andrews, George Reeves, Victor Mature, and Don DeFore. Even in the distinguished company of Playhouse veterans like Victor Jory and Samuel S. Hinds, young Preston Meservey - or Pres, as he was always known to his friends - was an acknowledged star in the making. During one play a Paramount scout saw him, and he signed a contract with the studio, which renamed him Robert Preston.

After three appearances in low-budget flicks, Robert first caught the public's attention with his performance in the railroad drama *Union Pacific* (1939) with Barbara Stanwyck. Also around this time, Preston had a supporting role as Digby Geste in *Beau Geste* (1939) with Gary Cooper and Ray Milland. After several other roles in inconsequential films, Preston became a favorite of director Cecil B. DeMille,who cast him in several films like *Reap the Wild Wind* (1942) and *Northwest Mounted Police* (1940).[11]

---

10 The Pasadena Playhouse was a great training ground for stage actors as well as future film stars like the ones mentioned. It was founded in 1916 and continues today as a starting place for new plays and musicals.

In 1946, after serving in England with the Army Air Corps, Preston married Kay Feltus (aka Catherine Craig) – to whom he was married for 47 years and whom he had known in Pasadena. He struggled through numerous unfulfilling roles in the 40s, then relocated to New York and concentrated on theatre.There, he appeared in several comedies, including "His and Hers" (1954) and "The Tender Trap"(1954). His great success, however, came as the charming charlatan "Professor" Harold Hill in "The Music Man." The plot focuses on Hill's arrival in River City and his attempt to scam the townspeople by convincing them to donate money for instruments for a children's band and then planning to run off with their funds. His plan hits a snag when he falls for Marian, the local librarian. The show ran for 1,375 performances and earned Preston a Tony Award for Best Actor in a Musical in 1958. He reprised his role as the con man for the 1962 film version with Shirley Jones playing Marian.

Continuing to work on stage and in films, Preston won his second Tony Award for :I Do! I Do!" starring opposite Mary Martin from 1966 to 1967. The musical explores one couple's 50 years of married life. A few years later, Preston was nominated for a Tony Award for his work on "Mack & Mabel" (1974). On the big screen, he had notable roles in the adaptation of the musical *Mamw* (1973) opposite Lucille Ball and *Semi-Tough* (1977). In the 1980s, he started working with director Blake Edwards. His work in 1981's *S.O.B.* was warmly received and he was nominated for an Academy Award for his performance as "Toddy," a gay nightclub entertainer, in *Victor/Victoria* (1982).

Preston passed away from lung cancer in 1987 at age 69.

Awards

Robert Preston was nominated for a Best Supporting Actor Oscar in 1982 for his performance in *Victor, Victoria* but lost out to Lou Gossett, Jr.

---

11 Like many actors, Preston did not particularly care for DeMille, who was not considered to be an actor's director.

Preston received Golden Globe nominations for "Victor, Victoria"and also for "The Music Man" in 1962. But his greatest recognition was the Tony Award which he won in 1958 for "The Music Man" and again in 1967 for "I Do! I Do!:He was also nominated for a Tony in 1975 for "Mack and Mabel," in which he played early movie producer and director Mack Sennett.

My Favorite Robert Preston Films
1. *The Music Man* - 1962
2. *Wake Island* – 1942
3. *Reap the Wild Wind* – 1942
4. *Beau Geste* – 1939
5. *Northwest Mounted Police* – 1940
6. *Union Pacific* - 1939

Admittedly, some of Robert Preston's best films were in the 60s, 70s, and 80s, but with one exception, I focused on those covered by the years included in this book.

1. *The Music Man* - 1962

Although technically outside the years covered by this book, how could I possibly ignore Robert Preston's career-defining performance as "Professor" Harold Hill in *The Music Man*!

Harold Hill (Preston), the con-man salesman who goes from small town to small town in the early 1900s selling the townsfolk a bill of goods in which he pockets their money and then skips town without delivering the goods, lands in a small Iowa town and pretends to be Professor Harold Hill of the Gary Conservatory of Music – class of '05. He promises to teach all the high school kids how to play an instrument, and of course, he charms their parents.

Things are going as they do normally until Hill falls in love with Marian, the town librarian (the lovely and talented Shirley Jones) who has a younger brother who does not talk much but who Hill takes a liking to.

Everything is proceeding as normal when it comes time for Hill and his pal Marcellus Washburn (Buddy Hackett) to skip out with the money, when suddenly Hill questions whether or not he wants to take off – you see, he has fallen in love not only with Marian but also the community in general, and he faces not only exposure but tar and feathering to boot if he stays. Of course, everything turns out just fine (it's a musical!) in this wonderful tale of early 20th century Americana.

The performances are terrific, not only by the three leads, but also by Paul Ford as the town mayor and Hermione Gingold as his wife, plus a young Ron Howard as Winthrop, Shirley Jones' brother. But it is the performance of Robert Preston, who was born to play this part, that makes *The Music Man* special.

The Music Man grossed $15 million, quite a sum in 1962!

Robert Preston as Professor Harold Hill, the best role of his career. He also played the part on Broadway before making the film.

Preston attempting to get Shirley Jones – Marian the Librarian – on his side in *The Music Man*.

2. *Wake Island* – 1942

In the early days of World War II, just before the attack on Pearl Harbor, Major Caton takes command of the small Marine garrison on Wake Island. His tendency toward spit and polish upsets the men's tropical laziness, but Pearl Harbor changes everything. Soon the island is attacked and the Marines pull together day by day; but how long can they hold out? [12]

---

12   In reality Wake Island was the site of Japan's first unsuccessful attack on American forces in the Battle of Wake Island when U.S. Marines and Navy forces repelled an attempted Japanese invasion, sinking two enemy destroyers and a transport. The island fell to overwhelming Japanese forces 12 days later in a second attack, this time with extensive support from Japanese carrier-based aircraft returning from the attack on Pearl Harbor, four days previously. Wake Island remained occupied by Japanese forces until the end of the war in 1945.

Good performances by all, including Brian Donlevy as Major Caton, plus Robert Preston, MacDonald Carey, and William Bendix, make this a better-than average war film. Major Caton quickly identifies Preston and Bendix as the two chief troublemakers, but of course they come around after the attack on Pearl Harbor.[13]

Wake Island was nominated for four academy awards, including Best Picture, Best Director, and Best Supporting Actor (Bendix), but did not win any. For best picture, it lost out to *Mrs. Miniver*, a WWII film from the British perspective.

3. *Reap the Wild Wind* – 1942

Robert Preston was a busy guy in 1942, making this Cecil B. DeMille spectacular as well as *Wake Island* and *This Gun for Hire* with Alan Ladd.

Reap the Wild Wind is one of my all-time favorite movies. Sure, it has the typical dopey DeMille dialogue, but the plot, action, special effects for 1942, and star quality are really good.

What a cast! Ray Milland, Paulette Goddard, John Wayne, and Susan Hayward. And that does not even include Raymond Massey and Robert Preston as the Cutler brothers!

---

13 While the names of the characters are fictional, the events depicted in the film are, of course, true. As you can imagine, the film was a big hit for a nation just entering into World War II.

In the 1840s in Key West, Florida, salvaging companies compete for the right to claim salvage from clipper ships that sink in the hazardous waters in and around Key West. Loxi Claiborne (Paulette Goddard) owns one of the salvage ships, but she seems to always lose out to the Cutler brothers (Raymond Massey and Robert Preston) because the Cutlers seem to find a way to make sure the ships run aground.

Loxie befriends the captain of one of the sunk ships, Jack Stuart (John Wayne) and nurses him back to health, where they begin a courtship. Shortly after that, she travels to Charleston, South Carolina to convince the shipping company and its lawyer, Stephen Tolliver (Ray Milland in a good role) that the Cutlers and not Jack Stuart are responsible for the sinking ship.

The rest of the film revolves around Tolliver conducting his own investigation to find the truth, with the help of Loxie and Jack Stuart (sometimes). When the steamship *Southern Cross* is sunk, and it appears that Robert Preston's girl friend (Susan Hayward) may have been a stowaway and lost her life, a trial ensues. In the exciting climax, Tolliver and Stuart agree to make the dive to determine if there was indeed a girl on board the sunken ship[14], and there is a fight to the finish with a giant squid in which only one of the heroes survives.

All the stars are really good in this film, including Preston, Milland, Massey, and Wayne (Susan Hayward really has a bit part in the film.) But it is clearly Paulette Goddard's film, and she excels as the glamorous tomboy.

> Paulette Goddard was the leading candidate for the role of Scarlet O'Hara until David O. Selznick discovered Vivien Leigh. But Goddard handles herself quite well in a similar role

---

14   Dan Cutler – Robert Preston – says he will "spill the beans" if the body of his sweetheart is found in the wrecked ship.

From this photo of Paulette Goddard with Ray Milland, you can envision that Goddard would have done quite nicely as Scarlett O'Hara if Vivien Leigh had not gotten the part.

Reap the Wild Wind won an Oscar for best special effects – not surprising – and was a huge box office success. It was released in early 1942 and served as nice escapism for a country that had just plunged into World War II. And it enhanced Preston's image as someone who could play heroes and villains with equal believability.

4. *Beau Geste* – 1939

Beau, John, and Digby Geste (Gary Cooper, Ray Milland, and Robert Preston) are three inseparable, adventurous brothers who were adopted as youngsters into the wealthy household of Lady Brandon. When they become young men and as money in the upper class household grows tight, Lady Brandon is forced to sell her most treasured jewel, the mighty "Blue Water" sapphire. The household gets it out for one final look, the lights go out, and it vanishes - stolen by one of the brothers, no doubt. That night, Beau, Digby, and John each "confess" and slip out, John leaving behind Isabel (Susan Hayward), whom he loves.

They all join the French Foreign Legion, and Beau and Digby are split from John and put under the command of the ruthless and sadistic

Sergeant Markoff (Brian Donlevy). Conditions continue to deteriorate as the rest of the Legionnaires plot a mutiny against Markoff, in the midst of an attack by Arab hordes. One of Markoff's tricks is to prop up the dead bodies of the legionnaires to give the attacking Arabs the impression that these men are still manning the fort.

We eventually find out which of the brothers actually stole the sapphire – of course, it had to be the leader, Beau. Also, only one of the three Geste brothers actually survives the attack – John, of course, because he has Susan Hayward waiting for him. At the very end of the film, Lady Brandon reads aloud Beau's letter, which reveals that he stole the gem because he knew it was a fake. Lady Brandon had sold the real one years before, and Beau wanted to protect her. As a child, he was hiding in a suit of armor and witnessed the transaction.

Beau Geste is a terrific adventure film, with Cooper, Milland, and Preston all in fine form and Donlevy a terrific villain (Donlevy was nominated for an Oscar for his performance). The film received critical acclaim as well as favorable public reviews. As in the previous film, Susan Hayward does not have much to do, and Donald O'Connor has a small part as young Beau.

The three Geste brothers – John, Beau, and Digby

5. *Northwest Mounted Police* – 1940

Yet another late 30s/early 40s Robert Preston flick, and another one directed by Cecil B. DeMille, which meant a good plot, good special effects, and dopey dialogue. And *Northwest Mounted Police* does not disappoint in any of those three categories.

Texas Ranger Dusty Rivers (Gary Cooper) travels to Canada in the 1880s in search of Jacques Corbeau (George Bancroft) , who is wanted for murder. He wanders into the midst of the Riel Rebellion, in which Métis (people of French and Native heritage) and Natives want a separate nation. Dusty falls for nurse April Logan (Madeleine Carroll), who is also loved by Mountie Jim Brett (Preston Foster).

April's brother Ronnie (Robert Preston, as a Canadian Mountie) is enamored with Courbeau's daughter Louvette (Paulette Goddard), which leads to trouble during the battles between the rebels and the Mounties. Ronnie is tricked into giving vital information to the outlaws on the Mounties' planned attack. Through it all Dusty is determined to bring Corbeau back to Texas.

Again, *Northwest Mounted Police* features an excellent cast, good action sequences, but not the best dialogue you could muster. This is the first of three pairings between Preston and DeMille, and also the first of three pairings between Paulette Goddard and DeMille, with *Unconquered* the third.[15]

The film opened in Regina, Saskatchewan, Canada in October 1940 and was Paramount's biggest hit of 1940. While it was a hit with the public, the critics were not that impressed. *Northwest Mounted Police* was nominated for five Oscars, but won only one, for Best Film Editing. DeMille narrated portions of the story, a practice he followed in other films, including *Reap the Wild Wind*.

---

15 Paulette Goddard got a big break in her career with this role. It is said she wanted the part so bad, she donned herself in dark skin make-up, put on an Indian get-up with feathers and walked into DeMille's office saying, "You teenk you wan beeg director, hah? Me, Louvette, show you!" And I guess she did!

I can see why Preston's character would fall for Paulette Goddard. That's Madeleine Carroll on the left.

6. *Union Pacific* - 1939

One of the last bills signed by President Lincoln authorizes pushing the Union Pacific Railroad across the wilderness to California. But financial opportunist Asa Barrows hopes to profit from obstructing it. Chief troubleshooter Jeff Butler (Joel McCrea) has his hands full fighting Barrows' agent, gambler Sid Campeau (Brian Donlevy, again as the no-good-nick); Campeau's partner Dick Allen (Robert Preston) is Jeff's war buddy and rival suitor for engineer's daughter Molly Monahan (Barbara Stanwyck). Who will survive the effort to push the railroad through at any cost?

Union Pacific, along with another 1939 film, *Stagecoach*, helped turn the western into a more adult genre. They both featured real adult challenges rather than just the routine shoot-em-ups. And this is another film where Robert Preston, still early in his career, plays second fiddle to more established stars like Gary Cooper, John Wayne, and Joel McCrea and acquits himself very well.

It is worthwhile to mention the name of character actor Lynne Overman here. Overman appeared in this film and was another DeMille favorite. He was outstanding as Captain Phillip Philpott in *Reap the Wild Wind*, who always seems to come up with a funny line at the perfect time.

Robert Preston was a gifted leading man who was also a very good actor. He was equally good, no matter whether the genre was a Western, drama, or adventure film. And he did his best work of all in the musical *The Music Man*. Truly a star worth remembering.

3. Greer Garson (1904-1996)

Greer Garson was a very popular and accomplished actress of the stage and screen, playing a variety of roles including *Mrs. Miniver*, Elizabeth Bennet in *Pride and Prejudice*, and Marie Curie in *Madame Curie*. Herpopularity in films was most pronounced during the 1940s, before, during, and after World War II. But she continued to get good movie roles into the 1960s and even made an appearance in *The Love Boat* television series in 1982 as her last credit. (That probably convinced her that enough was enough!)

Biography

A strikingly attractive, red-haired former stage actress of Anglo-Irish descent, Greer Garson appeared in 44 films and television shows beginning in 1939, mostly with MGM.

Eileen Evelyn Greer Garson was born on September 29, 1904 in London, England, to Nancy Sophia (Greer) and George Garson, a commercial clerk. She was of Scottish and Ulster-Scots descent. Her childhood was a normal if not non-descript life. Greer showed no early signs of interest in becoming an actress; instead she was educated at the University of London with the intention of becoming a teacher. However, after graduation she opted to work with an advertising agency. During this time, Greer Garson appeared in local theatrical productions gaining a reputation as an extremely talented actress. Discovered by **Louis B. Mayer** while he was on a visit to London looking for new talent., Garson was signed to a contract with MGM and appeared in her first American film in 1939.

Her relatively brief but excellent debut performance as Mrs. Chipping in the touching *Goodbye Mr. Chips* (1939) won her the first of seven Oscar nominations as Best Actress and made her an immediate star. After an impressive turn as the intelligent, playful Elizabeth Bennet in *Pride and Prejudice* (1940), Garson inherited from Norma Shearer the mantle of MGM's resident prestige actress, suffering with polite dignity through a series of A-budget soap operas and costume dramas.

Garson regularly appeared on box office polls of the top ten stars during the WWII years; indeed, Betty Grable was the only female star who surpassed Garson in popularity during this time.[16] Garson formed an attractive romantic cinema partnership with the stalwart and gentlemanly Walter Pidgeon, with whom she co-starred eight times. Their finest pairings came with *Madame Curie* (1943) and *ThatForsythe Woman* (1949), though their most recognizable pairing is as Mr. and *Mrs. Miniver* (1942), a tribute to the stiff-upper-lip spirit of the British in WWII, for which she won an Oscar. Garson also played quite well opposite popular matinee idols Ronald Colman in the touching, sentimental romance, *Random Harvest* (1942) and Gregory Peck in the lavish family saga, *The Valley of Decision* (1945).

---

16   Greer Garson biography from TCM

Garson's popularity began to ebb during the late 40s, with her regal and dignified stoicism during the war years seeming less suitable in the face of postwar realism. Some of the attempts to vary Garson's image and type of roles, such as in the zany farce *Julia Misbehaves* (1948), were not particularly successful, but she continued on into the middle of the following decade with such smaller-scale vehicles as *Scandal at Scourie* (1953) and *Strange Lady in Town* (1955). She later made a comeback with her acclaimed performance as Eleanor Roosevelt opposite Ralph Bellamy in *Sunrise at Campobello* (1960) and also did periodic stage work. Her last feature acting role was in 1967's *The Happiest Millionaire* and her final film appearance was in the documentary *Directed by William Wyler* (1986). Garson, who had worked sporadically in TV since the 1950s, made one of her last acting appearances as Aunt March in the miniseries *Little Women* (NBC, 1978). After dabbling briefly in theatrical producing (notably the New York production of "On Golden Pond"), she retired in 1980 after suffering a heart attack. Eight years later, she underwent bypass surgery. Garson succumbed to heart failure at age 92 on April 6, 1996.

The actress was married three times. Her second husband (1943-47) was actor Richard Ney, who had played her son in *Mrs. Miniver* and was 12 years younger than her.

Awards

Greer Garson was nominated for seven Best Actress Oscars, and won once, for *Mrs. Miniver* (1942) She was also nominated but did not win for the following films:[17]

Goodbye, Mr. Chips – 1939
Blossoms in the Dust – 1941
Madame Curie – 1943
Mrs. Parkington – 1944
The Valley of Decision – 1945
Sunrise at Campobello – 1960

My Favorite Greer Garson Films

---

17   That she was nominated seven times tells you how good an actress she was.

1. *Pride and Prejudice* – 1940
2. *Mrs. Miniver* – 1942
3. *Random Harvest* – 1942
4. *Goodbye, Mr. Chips* – 1939
5. *Strange Lady in Town* - 1955

1. *Pride and Prejudice* - 1940

The first screen version of the Jane Austen novel – one of my favorite novels – features Greer Garson as Elizabeth Bennet (the central figure in the book and movie) – and Laurence Oliver as Mr. Darcy. How can you possibly go wrong with that combination?

Sure, Garson is too old for the part – she was 35 when the movie was filmed, and Elizabeth Bennet is supposed to be about 19. But I never really noticed a problem with her character – she was just fabulous as the level-headed second sister in a family of mostly spoiled nutcases.

Mr. and Mrs. Bennet have five unmarried daughters, and Mrs. Bennet is especially eager to find suitable husbands for them - her sole concern in life, in fact. That is because women were not allowed to inherit their parent's estates at that time, so their home and its possessions would automatically go to their cousin, Mr. Collins, a bumbling fool who bases his entire life on what his aunt – Edna Mae Oliver in a wonderful performance as the snooty Lady Catherine de Bourgh - thinks about anything. When the rich single gentlemen Mr. Bingley and Mr. Darcy come to live nearby, the Bennets have high hopes. But her pride, Darcy's prejudice against people he believes are beneath him, and misunderstandings all combine to complicate their relationships and make happiness difficult. At times, the viewer believes that Elizabeth and Darcy are never going to get together.

The cast is simply outstanding, with Maureen O'Sullivan as Elizabeth's older sister Jane, the other level-headed sister – and Edmund Gwen (Santa Clause in *Miracle on 34th Street*) – as their sensible father.

Special credit should go to two of the supporting players – Edna Mae Oliver as Catherine, who detests Elizabeth through most of the film, and Melville Cooper as the reverend Mr. Collins, who will inherit the Bennet estate upon the death of Mr. Bennet.

The great Edna Mae Oliver as Lady Catherine, with Greer Garson in *Pride and Prejudice*. She looks like something out of Alice in Wonderland.

Melville Cooper as Mr. Collins. Don't you just want to slap this guy?

By the way, Melville Cooper had a knack for playing blundering, cowardly characters, most notably as the ineffectual Sheriff of Nottingham in the 1938 classic, *Adventures of Robin Hood*, with Errol Flynn in his signature role. But Cooper could also play gangsters and con men.

In real life Cooper served in World War I as a lieutenant with the

Seaforth Highlanders, a noted Scottish regiment, and was wounded and taken prisoner by the Germans. So there!

Pride and Prejudice won one Oscar, for Cedric Gibbons for Best Art Direction, one of 11 Best Art Direction Oscars won by the accomplished Mr. Gibbons.

2. *Mrs. Miniver* – 1942

Mrs. Miniver tells the story of a middle-class English family attempting to survive the early days of World War II, when bombings by the German air force were almost a daily fact of life.[18] While dodging bombs, the Minivers' son courts Lady Beldon's granddaughter. In spite of the war, the English people try to keep their daily lives as much intact as possible. One example is the annual rose competition, where a rose is named after Mrs. Miniver and entered in the competition against Lady Beldon (who always wins the competition.)

More than just another film, *Mrs. Miniver* did a great deal to inform the American people about Britain's defiance against Nazi Germany and the steadfast resolution of the British people in the face of seemingly overwhelming odds. Coming at a time of heightened emotions - as well as being expertly produced and extremely well acted - it is easy to see why the film earned six Oscars, including Best Picture & Best Director (William Wyler), Best Actress (Greer Garson), and Best Supporting Actress (Teresa Wright as the aforementioned granddaughter.)

3. *Random Harvest* – 1942

1942 was a very good year for Greer Garson, as both *Mrs. Miniver* and *Random Harvest* were released that year.

At the close of World War I, a shell-shocked amnesia victim (Ronald Colman) is sequestered in a London sanitarium; with no identity and no next of kin, he has nowhere else to go. Unable to stand the loneliness, Colman wanders into the streets, then stumbles into a music hall, where he is befriended by a good-natured entertainer (Greer Garson). That Colman and Garson fall in love and marry should surprise no one; what is surprising, at least to Colman, is that he discovers that he has a talent for writing. Three years pass: while in Liverpool to sell one of his stories, Colman is struck down by a speeding car. When he comes to,

---

18 Remember, this was before America entered WWII.

he has gained full memory of his true identity; alas, he has completely forgotten both Garson and their child. Returning to his well-to-do relatives, Colman takes over the family business.

Having lost her child, the distraught Garson seeks out the missing Colman. A psychiatrist (Philip Dorn) helps Garson, advising her that to reveal her identity may prove a fatal shock for her husband. To stay near him, Garson takes a job as Colman's secretary. "Strangely" attracted to Garson, Colman falls in love with her all over again. Will there be yet another memory lapse? Under normal circumstances, we wouldn't believe a minute of *Random Harvest*, but the chemistry and acting skills of the two stars transform this unlikely premise into a completely inspiring film.

Colman and Garson are perfectly cast for the film (although he is a bit old to be a young war veteran). The film was one of MGM's biggest hits in 1942 - indeed, one of the biggest in the studio's history. Nominated for seven Oscars, including Best Picture and Best Actor for Ronald Colman, it did not win any. [19]

4. *Goodbye, Mr. Chips* – 1939

Goodbye, Mr. Chips tells the story of a somewhat stodgy old classics teacher (Robert Donat in the title role of Charles Edward Chipping) who looks back over his long career, remembering pupils and colleagues, and above all the idyllic courtship and marriage that transformed his life. It blends the plot around several actual historical events, including the death of Queen Victoria, the invention of the telephone, and World War I, which Chips erroneously states will not last for more than a month.

Greer Garson has a small but important role as his wife, who he meets on a holiday in Austria and marries. Unfortunately, while she dies in childbirth, her positive effect on Chips lasts for the remainder of his life.

By the way, Robert Donat very ably handles the complex role of Chips through the years, from about his mid-20s until his 80s. To demonstrate how good he was, he beat out a fellow named Clark Gable for the Best Actor Oscar; Gable happened to play Rhett Butler in *Gone with the Wind*.

---

19 Greer Garson won the Best Actress Oscar, but for *Mrs. Miniver*.

Greer Garson and Robert Donat in *Goodbye, Mr. Chips*

5. *Strange Lady in Town* – 1955

Certainly not a great film, but I liked it. The idea of Greer Garson in a Western is at the same time preposterous but charming.

In 1880 New Mexico, a young female doctor from Boston (Greer Garson) arrives in Santa Fe to establish her new medical practice. Dr. Julia Garth is set to live with her brother, U.S. Cavalry lieutenant David Garth (Cameron Mitchell). The town already has a male physician, Dr. Rourke O'Brien (the always-good Dana Andrews).

However, these were times when female doctors were almost unheard of. Some people even considered it a shameful offense for a woman to be a doctor, and that women's roles should be limited to the minding of the household and the rearing of children. In addition, she plans on bringing modern medical methods to New Mexico. Therefore, her methods are consistently challenged by the conservative element of the town as well as by Dr. O'Brien. But after a couple of tragedies, the good doctor(s) get together as we knew they would.

Dana Andrews and Greer Garson appear to be getting along in this scene. Andrews is one of my favorite all-time movie stars.[20]

Greer Garson was a British-American actress who was extremely popular during the Second World War, being listed by the *Motion Picture Herald* as one of America's top-ten box office draws from 1942 to 1946. She was nominated for seven Best Actress Oscars, including five in a row between 1941 and 1945, and won for *Mrs. Miniver*.

After basically retiring from acting, she was married to a Texas oilman – E.E. Fogleman – for almost 40 years and became a breeder of horses as well as a philanthropist. As a result, during her later years, Garson was recognized for her philanthropy and civic leadership. She donated several million dollars for the construction of the Greer Garson Theatre at both the Santa Fe University of Art and Design and at Southern Methodist University's Meadows School of the Arts. Also a registered Republican, she was offered the opportunity to run for Congress in 1966 in Texas but declined.

As you can see, Greer Garson was much more than just a movie star.

---

20   Andrews starred in two of the best films of all time, *The Best Years of Our Lives* and *Laura*.

4. Maureen O'Hara(1920-2015)

Maureen O'Hara was a beautiful and talented movie star whose career lasted for 62 years, between 1938 and 2000. She was most associated with John Wayne and starred with him in five films[21], including *The Quiet Man*. But O'Hara was also in many other classic films, including *Miracle on 34th Street* and *The Hunchback of Notre Dame*.

Biography

Though we know her as Maureen O'Hara, Maureen FitzSimons was born on August 17, 1920, in Ranelagh (a suburb of Dublin), Ireland. Her mother, Marguerita Lilburn FitzSimons, was an accomplished contralto singer. Her father, Charles FitzSimons,managed a business in Dublin and also owned part of the renowned Irish soccer team "The

---

21 *Rio Grande, The Quiet Man, The Wings of Eagles, McLintock,* and *Big Jake.*

Shamrock Rovers." Maureen was the second of six FitzSimons children in this very normal and happy family.

Maureen excelled in sports as a young girl. She combined this interest with an equally natural gift for performing. This talent was demonstrated by her winning pretty much every Feis award for drama and theatrical performing her country offered[22]. By age 14 she was accepted to the prestigious Abbey Theater and pursued her dream of classical theater and operatic singing. This course was to be altered, however, when actor Charles Laughton, after seeing a screen test of Maureen, became mesmerized by her beauty. Before casting her to star in *Jamaica Inn*(1939), Laughton and his partner, Erich Pommer, changed her name from Maureen FitzSimons to "Maureen O'Hara" - a bit shorter last name for the marquee.

Under contract to Laughton, Maureen's next picture was to be filmed in America (*The Hunchback of Notre Dame* (1939)) at RKO Pictures. The epic film was an extraordinary critical and box office success and Maureen's contract was eventually bought from Laughton by RKO Pictures. At 19, Maureen had already starred in two major motion pictures with Laughton. Unlike most stars of her era, she started at the top, and remained there for the remainder of her long career.

Maureen O'Hara had an enviable string of all-time classics to her credit that include *How Green Was My Valley* (1941), *Miracle on 34th Street* (1947), *Sitting Pretty* (1948), *The Quiet Man* (1952), *The Parent Trap* (1961) and *McLintock!* (1963). Add to this the distinction of being voted one of the five most beautiful women in the world and you have a film star who was as gorgeous as she was talented.

Although at times early in her career Hollywood didn't seem to notice, there was much more to Maureen O'Hara than her dynamic beauty.She not only had a wonderful lyric soprano voice, but she could use her inherent athletic ability to perform physical feats that most actresses couldn't begin to attempt, from fencing to fisticuffs. She was truly a natural athlete.

In her career Maureen starred with some of Hollywood's most dashing

---

22 An organized dance competition in Ireland. In Ireland, "feis" means "festival."

leading men, including Tyrone Power, John Payne, Rex Harrison, James Stewart, Henry Fonda, Brian Keith, and Sir Alec Guinness.Of course, her most famous pairing was with her good friend, John Wayne. She starred in five films with Wayne, the most beloved being *The Quiet Man*(1952). She also worked with some great directors, including (of course) John Ford, Alfred Hitchcock, William Dieterle, Henry Hathaway, Henry King, Jean Renoir, and William Wellman.

After two unsuccessful marriages, in 1968 she married Charles Blair. General Blair was a famous aviator whom she had known as a friend of her family for many years. Blair was the real-life version of what John Wayne had been on the screen. He had been a Brigadier General in the Air Force, a Senior Pilot with Pan American, and held many incredible record-breaking aeronautical achievements.With Blair, Maureen managed Antilles Airboats, a commuter sea plane service in the Caribbean. She not only made trips around the world with her pilot husband, but owned and published a magazine, *The Virgin Islander*, writing a monthly column called "Maureen O'Hara Says."

Tragically, Charles Blair died in a plane crash in 1978. Though completely devastated, Maureen recovered and was elected President and CEO of Antilles Airboats, which brought her the distinction of being the first woman president of a scheduled airline in the United States.

Supposedly retired from movie making and living in Boise, Idaho, she was coaxed out of retirement several times - once in 1991 to star with John Candy in *Only the Lonely* (1991) and again, in 1995, in a made-for-TV movie, *The Christmas Box* (1995) on CBS.

Maureen O'Hara passed away from natural causes on October 24, 2015 at the age of 95. One more thing: To anyone who says that there was no special friendship between John Wayne and Maureen O'Hara, I offer the following quote from Maureen: On May 21, 1979, she sat somberly at a table before the House Banking, Finance, and Urban Affair Subcommittee on Consumer Affairs. Her mission was bittersweet. Knowing her dear friend, John Wayne, was gravely ill, she had flown in from her home in St. Croix, the Virgin Islands, to give testimony for an authorization for the President of the United States to create a commemorative gold medal in his honor. Her flight had been cancelled into Washington, and she had come through New York instead. It was a harried day, and she hadn't even had a chance to make a prepared statement.

Instead, she just said, "I have known John Wayne for 39 years, and in those 39 years I have called him my dearest friend — my best friend ... To the people of the world, John Wayne is not just an actor — and a very fine actor — John Wayne IS the United States of America."

Awards

In November, 2014 Maureen O'Hara was honored by receiving a long overdue Oscar for "Lifetime Achievement" at the annual Motion Picture Arts and Sciences Governors Awards, the special awards given out separately from the regular Academy Awards.

My Favorite Maureen O'Hara Films

1. *The Quiet Man* (1952)
2. *Miracle on 34th Street* (1947)
3. *The Hunchback of Notre Dame* (1939)
4. *The Black Swan* (1942)
5. *Rio Grande* (1950)

1. *The Quiet Man* - 1952

The Quiet Man is a beautiful film directed by John Ford and starring John Wayne, but it is not a western! American boxer Sean Thornton (John Wayne) has returned from America to reclaim his homestead and escape his past life as a prize fighter[23]. Sean's eye is caught by Mary Kate Danaher (Maureen O'Hara), a beautiful but poor maiden, and younger sister of ill-tempered "Red" Will Danaher, (Victor McLaglen). The riotous relationship that forms between Sean and Mary Kate, punctuated by Will's pugnacious attempts to keep them apart, form the main plot, with Sean's past as the dark undercurrent.

The main plot is Will Danaher's refusal to give his sister her rightful dowry.Sean, unschooled in Irish customs, cares nothing about the dowry, but to Mary Kate the dowry represents her independence,

---

23   He killed a man in the ring.

identity, and pride. She feels passionately and intensely that the dowry is hers and is needed to validate her marriage to Sean. So the issue of the dowry must be resolved before Sean and Mary Kate can be married. This results in a long brawl between Wayne and MacLaglen after the dowry is paid off.

The Quiet Man is truly a wonderful film, beautifully photographed, with great acting and directing. I can't imagine anyone but Wayne and O'Hara playing the two leads. And the supporting cast of Irish actors, including McLaglen, Barry Fitzgerald, Ward Bond as a priest, and Arthur Shields (Fitzgerald's brother in real life) are all perfectly cast. *The Quiet Man* won Oscars for John Ford as Best Director, and also for Best Cinematography (no surprise) and was nominated for five other Oscars, including best picture and best supporting actor (McLaglen). [24]

Barry Fitzgerald (left) and Arthur Shields. They do look like brothers, but Fitzgerald was eight years older and much more well known. By the way, the family name was actually Shields.

2. *Miracle on 34th Street* - 1947

At Macy's Department Store's Thanksgiving Day parade in downtown New York City, the fellow playing Santa is discovered by an old man to be drunk on the job and is fired. Doris Walker (Maureen O'Hara), the

---

24   In the best picture category, it lost out to *The Greatest Show on Earth*, which was nowhere near as good as this film or *High Noon*.

blunt and humorless special events director, persuades the old man (Edmund Gwenn in his most famous role) to take his place. He proves to be a sensation and is quickly recruited to be the store Santa at the main Macy's hub.

While the new Santa is successful, Ms. Walker learns that he calls himself Kris Kringle and that he claims to be the actual Santa Claus. Despite reassurances by Kringle's doctor that he is harmless, Doris still has misgivings, especially when she has cynically trained herself, and especially her daughter, Susan (a nine-year -old Natalie Wood), to reject all notions of belief and fantasy.

However, people, especially Susan, begin to notice there is something special about Kris and his determination to advance the true spirit of Christmas amidst the rampant commercialism around him. When a raucous conflict with the store's cruelly incompetent psychologist erupts, Kris hits him over the head with an umbrella, which leads to Kris' confinement in a psychiatric hospital. Kris and his attorney (John Payne) must prove to the judge that he is the real Santa Claus.

Everything about this film - cast, story, and direction - is first rate. O'Hara, Payne, and Wood are perfectly cast, but it is Edmund Gwenn as Kris Kringle who steals the movie. Not only does he look like Santa Claus, he is extremely positive and likeable. An excellent supporting cast includes Porter Hall[25] as the psychiatrist, Gene Lockhart as the judge, Jerome Cowen (Humphrey Bogart's ill-fated partner in *The Maltese Falcon*), as the defense attorney, and William Frawley (Fred Mertz from *I Love Lucy* fame) as a political advisor to the judge.

The film won three Oscars - Edmund Gwenn for Best Supporting Actor - surprise, surprise!), Best Writing (Original Story) and Best Writing (Screenplay); It was also nominated for Best Picture but lost out to *Gentleman's Agreement*, with Gregory Peck. If you are not brought to tears by the very last scene in the film, there is something seriously wrong with you - that is all I will say!

---

25   Porter Hall was the murderer in the original *Thin Man* film.

Maureen O'Hara, Edmund Gwenn, and Natalie Wood, in *Miracle on 34th Street.* Tell me that's not the real Santa Claus in that pic!

3. *The Hunchback of Notre Dame* - 1939

The Hunchback of Notre Dame was Maureen O'Hara's second starring role in films (*Jamaica Inn* was first) since being discovered by Charles Laughton. This is the first sound version of the great Victor Hugo novel and was a huge hit.[26]

The movie is a fictional account of Paris in the 15th century. In the film, King Louis XI is a wise king[27] and Frollo (Cedric Hardwicke) is his Chief Justice who dispenses "justice" to the citizenry. Frollo sees the

---

26 The 1923 silent film version, starring Lon Chaney, is still probably the best version of the film, primarily because Chaney was terrific in the part.

27 In reality Louis XI was a schemer and was known as the "Spider King" because he was always spinning webs of intrigue.

gypsy girl, Esmeralda (Maureen O'Hara), in the church during Fool's Day, is mesmerized by her beauty, and sends the hunchbacked Quasimodo (Charles Laughton) to catch her. Quasimodo, with the girl in tow, is then captured by Phoebus (Alan Marshal), Captain of the Guards, who frees the girl. The courts sentence Quasimodo to be flogged, and the only one who will give him water while he is tied in the square is Esmeralda.

The subplot of this film includes Frollo's attempt to rid Paris of gypsies, who are persecuted and technically prohibited from entering Paris. (They do, anyway, and form an underground community - both figuratively and literally).

Later, at a party of nobles, Esmeralda again encounters both Frollo and Phoebus. When Phoebus is stabbed to death, Esmeralda is accused of the murder, convicted by the court and sentenced to hang. Clopin (Thomas Mitchell), King of the Beggars; Gringoire (a very thin Edmond O'Brien), who eventually becomes Esmeralda's husband; and Quasimodo, the bell ringer of the cathedral of Notre Dame, all try different ways to save her from the gallows, but only Quasimodo, the Hunchback, who brings her into the cathedral, is successful in saving her.

The cast includes some very fine actors, including Hardwicke, O'Brien, and Mitchell, but Laughton as Quasimodo and O'Hara as Esmeralda steal the show. Only 19 when she made this film, her incredible beauty captures the attention of virtually all the males in the cast, and her performance is very believable. She is the centerpiece of the film and acquits herself very well.

> One name that even classic film fans may not recognize is Alan Marshal, who played Phoebus, the handsome captain of the guards. An Australian, he was sort of a poor man's Errol Flynn, who was a fellow Aussie (actually a Tasmanian). He never quite became a star and eventually returned to his first love, the theater.

Suave leading man Alan Marshal. He was the murderer that Perry Mason defended in one of only two cases that Perry Mason lost in the long-running television series. But, in Perry's defense, it was a case of mistaken identity that fooled him until the finale. The episode was *The Case of the Terrified Typist*.

4. *The Black Swan* - 1942

I am a huge fan of swashbucklers/swordplay movies, and *The Black Swan* is one of the better ones. After England and Spain make peace, notorious pirateHenry Morgan (Laird Cregar in another good role) decides to reform. As a reward, he is made Governor of Jamaica, with a mandate to rid the Caribbean of his former pirate comrades, by persuasion if possible or by force if necessary. He replaces the former governor, Lord Denby (George Zucco), but is not trusted by either the lawful residents or the pirates.

Captain Jamie Waring (Tyrone Power) and his lieutenant, Tom Blue (Thomas Mitchell), reluctantly give up their piracy out of friendship for Morgan, but others in the Pirate Brotherhood, such as Captain Billy

Leech (George Sanders) and Wogan (Anthony Quinn), refuse to change.

Meanwhile, Waring takes a liking to Denby's daughter, Lady Margaret (Maureen O'Hara), who happens to be inconveniently engaged to an English gentleman, Roger Ingram (Edward Ashley). As it turns out, her fiancé is secretly providing information about ship sailings to the unrepentant pirates. Countless adventures ensue, and Power and O'Hara end up together - of course.

In addition to being a darn good swashbuckler, Maureen O'Hara is much more than merely a damsel in constant distress. She plays an active role in helping the good guys - former pirates - against the bad guys - current pirates.

> While Henry Morgan was perhaps the most famous pirate of his era, he is perhaps best known today for the brand of rum named after him. Captain Morgan rum was introduced by Seagram in 1944 and remains a popular brand of rum to this day.

5. *Rio Grande* - 1950

Rio Grande is the last of the three films in what has become known as the John Ford/John Wayne cavalry trilogy that also included *Fort Apache* and *She Wore a Yellow Ribbon*, but the only one of the three that Maureen O'Hara appeared in.

Rio Grande takes place after the Civil War when the Union turned its attention West towards the Apache Indians. Union officer Kirby Yorke (John Wayne) is in charge of an outpost on the Rio Grande River in which he is in charge of training new recruits, one of which is his son Jefferson (Claude Jarman, Jr.) whom he has not seen in 15 years. He whips him into shape to take on the Apaches but not before his mother Kathleen (Maureen O'Hara) shows up to take him out of there by buying him out of his enlistment. The decision to leave is left up to the young man, who decides to stay and fight. Through it all Kirby and Kathleen, though separated for years, fall back in love and decide that it is time to give their marriage another try. But Yorke faces his toughest battle when his unorthodox plan to outwit the elusive Apaches leads to possible court martial. Locked in a bloody Indian war, he must fight to redeem his honor and save the love and lives of his family.

Rio Grande is an excellent Western, with Wayne at his heroic best and O'Hara as his estranged wife who comes back into his life after a long absence. The supporting cast includes Ben Johnson and Harry Carey, Jr. as the two soldiers assigned to look after the younger Yorke, and Victor McLaglen as Sergeant Major Timothy Quincannon, the grumpy trainer of the new recruits.

The film features superb photography, wonderful acting, and the usual outstanding direction of John Ford, who embraces many of his typical themes - friendship and camaraderie of those who are forced together in a common bond, family, and a nice blend of humor with terrific action scenes.

John Wayne, Maureen O'Hara, and Claude Jarman, Jr. in *Rio Grande*.

Rio Grande was the first film appearance of 21 year old Patrick Wayne, John Wayne's second oldest son. Patrick Wayne would go on to appear in over 70 films and television shows, but never really became a star.

Maureen O'Hara was a rare combination of beauty, brains, and solid acting talent. While she will always be remembered for any number of quality motion pictures, her co-starring efforts with longtime friend John Wayne will always stand out in my mind.

5. Robert Mitchum (1917-1997)

With over 130 acting credits in his long career, Robert Mitchum was an under-rated actor with an independent spirit who never seemed to take acting too seriously and yet was very good at it. When asked one time what was his secret to acting, he said something like "I learn my lines, I come in, I say my lines, and I go home." On screen and off, he was noted for his casual indifference, as the above comment suggests. One of the two leading men actors of his era with a dimpled chin - the other was Kirk Douglas - Mitchum was a powerful presence in just about all his films. He was also quite happy to play an occasional villain, as he did so well in *Cape Fear* and especially *Night of the Hunter*; he typically played loners and drifters even in his romantic lead roles.

Biography

Robert Mitchum was an underrated American leading man of enormous ability, who seemed never to be all that interested in acting. He was born in Bridgeport, Connecticut, to Ann Harriet (Gunderson), a Norwegian immigrant, and James Thomas Mitchum, a shipyard/railroad worker. His father died in a train accident when Mitchum was two[28], and Robert and his siblings (including brother John Mitchum, later also an actor) were raised by his mother and stepfather (a British army major) in Connecticut, New York, and Delaware. An early contempt for authority - probably from an overly stern stepfather - led to discipline problems (including being expelled from middle school for fighting with a school principal), and the result was that Mitchum spent good portions of his teen years riding railroad cars. On one of these trips, at the age of 14, he was charged with vagrancy and sentenced to a Georgia chain gang, from which he escaped. Working a wide variety of jobs (including ghostwriter for astrologist Carroll Righter), Mitchum moved to California to live with his sister, who encouraged him to join a local theater group; there, Mitchum started as a stagehand and bit player and discovered acting in a Long Beach, California, amateur theater company. In the interim, he returned to Delaware and married his girl friend, Dorothy Spence.[29]

Back in California, Robert got a job as a machine operator at Lockheed Aircraft, where job stress caused him to suffer temporary blindness. So he turned to work as an extra in films. Then he began to obtain small roles in movies, appearing in dozens within a very brief time. In 1945, he was cast as Lt. Walker in *Story of G.I. Joe* and received an Oscar nomination as Best Supporting Actor. From then on, his star ascended rapidly, and he became an icon of 1940s film noir, though equally adept at westerns and romantic dramas. His apparently lazy style and seen-it-all demeanor proved highly attractive to audiences, and by the 1950s, he was a true superstar despite a brief prison term for marijuana usage in 1949, which seemed to enhance rather than diminish his "bad boy" appeal. [30]

Though seemingly dismissive of film as a form of "art," he worked in

---

28 Interesting. Barbara Stanwyck's mother died in a subway accident when she was four.

29 Despite his numerous affairs, the couple remained married for 57 years until Mitchum's death in 1997.

30 On the other hand, the career of his co-conspirator, Lila Leeds (who?) went downhill after her arrest for marijuana possession.

many thoughtful films, such as Charles Laughton's *The Night of the Hunter* (1955 and *Out of the Past* (1947). A master of accents and seemingly unconcerned about his image, he rarely played the typical hero but preferred playing flawed characters. Once in his 60s, Mitchum moved into television in the 1980s as his film opportunities diminished, winning new fans with *The Winds of War* (1983) and *War and Remembrance*(1988). His last film was *James Dean: Race with Destiny* (1997) with Casper Van Dien as James Dean.

Robert Mitchum died just short of his 80th birthday in 1997 of lung cancer and emphysema. Several of his family members also became actors.

Throughout his life, Mitchum was known as an avid reader and a bit of a renaissance man. On the one hand, he wrote poetry, songs, recorded two albums and once reportedly penned the libretto (text set to music) for an event Orson Welles directed at the Hollywood Bowl. On the other hand, he could be an intimidating man of contradictions: surly and charming, aloof and outgoing, humble and arrogant, pugnacious and gentle. I remember one interview that Robert Osborne did with Mitchum on Turner Classic Movies where Mitchum was just being a jerk throughout the entire interview, and Osborne later said it was the most trying interview he had ever done. However, I also remember another Osborne interview with Robert and good friend Jane Russell that went extremely well - both were very honest and good conversationalists.

Awards

Robert Mitchum was nominated for an Oscar for Best Supporting Actor for the 1945 film *The Story of G.I. Joe*. He received several Laurel awards[31] throughout his career as Best Male Star and also received the Cecil B. DeMille award at the Golden Globes in 1992.

My Favorite Robert Mitchum Films

Since he made so many good films, this is a tough choice. However, I will go with the following films from the 30s, 40s, and 50s (and a couple of good ones from the 60s also - out of the time period, I

---

31 An award given to those who advance the art of cinema.

apologize). Again, these are MY favorite Mitchum films, but not all of them are the BEST Robert Mitchum movies.

1. *The Night of the Hunter* (1955)
2. *Out of the Past* (1947)
3. *Holiday Affair* (1949)
4. *River of No Return* (1954)
5. *El Dorado* (1967)
6. *Cape Fear* (1962)
7. *Angel Face* (1953)

1. *The Night of the Hunter* - 1952

The Night of the Hunter is probably Robert Mitchum's single best performance on the big screen. His portrayal of preacher/con man Harry Powell is chilling and scary. I can't believe he was not given a Best Actor Oscar nomination, but that's Hollywood for you. He might not have been quite as good as Ernest Borgnine, the Oscar winner for his portrayal of Marty, the loveable loser butcher in *Marty*, but he was far superior to James Cagney in *Love Me or Leave Me* as an example.

During the great Depression of the 1930s, Ben Harper (a young Peter Graves) kills two people during a bank robbery, in which he stole and hid $10,000. Before he is captured, he is able to convince his adolescent son John and his daughter Pearl not to tell anyone, including their mother Willa (Shelly Winters), where he hid the money, namely in Pearl's favorite toy, a doll that she carries everywhere with her. Ben, who is tried and convicted, is sentenced to death. But before he is executed, Ben is in the state penitentiary with a cell mate, a man by the name of Harry Powell (Robert Mitchum), a self-professed man of the cloth, who is really a con man and murderer, swindling lonely women - primarily rich widows - of their money before he kills them. Since Ben will not tell Harry where he hid the money, after Ben's execution, Harry decides that Willa will be his next mark, figuring that someone in the family knows where the money is hidden. Willa ends up being easy prey for Harry's charismatic demeanor; soon he disposes of Willa and seeks out her two kids, who have run for their lives to get away from him.

The rest of the film centers around Harry's pursuit of Ben and Willa's two children, who end up in a rural home where an older woman

(Lillian Gish) takes in stray children - remember, this is the Great Depression. The plot involves her efforts to keep the two kids out of the clutches of the psychopathic Harry Powell, and results in many chilling and action-packed scenes.

Night of the Hunter is brilliantly directed by none other than Charles Laughton in the only movie he ever directed. [32] Mitchum is scary good as the psychopathic Harry Powell, who alternates between con man and killer. As viewers we are truly afraid for these two kids and Mitchum's unrelenting pursuit of them.

> Charles Laughton, who thought that Robert Mitchum was "one of the best actors in the world," wrote in *Esquire* of the private man heknew to be different than the public image: "All this tough talk is a blind, you know. He's a literate, gracious, kind man, with wonderful manners, and he speaks beautifully--when he wants to. He's a tender man and a very great gentleman. You know, he's really terribly shy." Laughton was usually ill at ease with very macho men yet very comfortable with his star on this film.

While Mitchum is almost as good as the crazy killer in *Cape Fear*, this film is probably the single best performance of his career. The viewer is afraid for the two kids in this film and realizes that Harry Powell will do anything, including committing murder, to get that money.

---

32 Mitchum was quoted as saying that he would work for Charles Laughton any time, that his experience on this film was very satisfying. On the other hand, Mitchum did not think all that much of Shelly Winters.

Robert Mitchum as Harry Powell in *Night of the Hunter*. You can see he is pretty creepy just by looking at this photo. He might really love something, but if so, it is money.

2. *Out of the Past* - 1947

Robert Mitchum was also really good in film noir thrillers, and this is probably his best effort in that genre.[33]

Jeff Bailey (Robert Mitchum), a gas station attendant in a small town in California, has his shadowy past catch up with him one day when he is ordered to meet with gambler Whit Sterling (Kirk Douglas). En route to the meeting, he tells his girlfriend Ann his story in a flashback. Years ago, Jeff was a private investigator hired by Sterling to find his mistress Kathie (Jane Greer), who shot Whit and made off with $40,000 of Sterling's money[34]. Jeff traces Kathie to Acapulco, Mexico, where the adorable Kathie uses her charms to make Jeff forget all about Sterling. However, when Jeff's former partner (Steve Brodie), finds the couple living in an isolated cabin out in the middle of nowhere, Kathie kills him and Jeff buries his corpse. Jeff accidentally finds the receipt of the bank deposit of the amount of money she stole in Kathie's purse and leaves her forever - so he says.

---

33   Film Noiris a cinematic term used primarily to describe stylish Hollywood crime dramas, particularly those which emphasize cynical attitudes, darkness, and sexual motivations. It also helped to have a "femme fatale" in the movie.

34   Worth almost $500,000 today.

Now back in the present, when Jeff meets Whit, he surprisingly finds Kathie living with him; Whit asks Jeff to perform one last job to get even and release Jeff from his debt. But Jeff finds that Whit is actually framing him. The rest of the film involves more intrigue and a series of double crosses.

Out of the Past meets all of the requirements of film noir - crime drama, cynical attitudes, darkness, and sexual motivations, and it definitely has a femme fatale in Jane Greer. In fact, it is one of the best film noirs of all time, thanks to a superb plot and the acting of Mitchum and Jane Greer. And it was made during a two-year period (1946 and 1947) where young Kirk Douglas played the heavy in this and two other films - *The Strange Love of Martha Ivers* and *I Walk Alone*, a terrific crime drama with Burt Lancaster in an unforgettable role.

> Jane Greer was another one of those actresses who should have been a big star but never quite made it to the A-list category. She was discovered by Howard Hughes at age 18 after he saw her on the cover of *Life* Magazine.

Robert Mitchum and Jane Greer in *Out of the Past*. Just by looking at this photo, I can tell he's in trouble. And I can tell she IS trouble.

3. *Holiday Affair* - 1949

Holiday Affair is a very under-appreciated Christmas film that somewhat reminds me of *Miracle on 34th Street* without Santa Claus. As usual, Robert Mitchum plays a likeable but offbeat character who sticks his nose in everyone else's business, with good intentions, of course.

Steve Mason (Robert Mitchum), a veteran and a drifter, is employed as a clerk during the Christmas season at Crowley's, a New York department store. He suspects customer Connie Ennis (Janet Leigh) of being a comparative shopper for a rival store when she buys an expensive toy train set without asking a single question about it. That night, her seven-year-old son Timmy (Gordon Gebert) becomes excited when he sneaks a peek at what he thinks is his Christmas present, only to be disappointed when his mother sets him straight. When Connie returns the train the next day, Steve tells her of his suspicions and that he should report her to the store detective, which would lead to her being fired from her job. After she explains that she is a war widow with a son to support, Steve refunds her money, a gesture that costs him his job at Crowley's.

Steve becomes acquainted with Connie, her son, and her longtime steady suitor, reliable but colorless lawyer Carl Davis (Wendell Corey). On Christmas morning, Timmy discovers the train set outside the apartment door and assumes that his mother got it for him after all. When Connie realizes who it must have come from, she finds the almost-broke Steve in Central Park, gives him a tie (originally intended for Carl), and offers to reimburse him for the expensive present. He refuses her money, saying that he wants to encourage Timmy's optimism. Connie then reveals she is marrying Carl on New Year's Day; Steve lets her know he thinks her decision is a mistake - it is obvious she does not love him, but that she is doing it for security for herself and her son. Annoyed, Connie goes home.

A series of adventures ensues revolving around the train, the Christmas present of a tie, and building toy boats, which is what Steve really wants to do with his life. Pursued by two men, which one will Connie choose? HINT: Do you really think she is going to choose Wendell Corey?

Mitchum is good as always in his role of a dreamer who just wants himself, Connie, and especially Timmy to be happy. And Janet Leigh is gorgeous as the comparison shopper/mom who is torn between Steve, Carl, and her dead husband. When Timmy tells her that he worries about what will happen to her when he grows up, gets married, and moves away, she really begins to rethink her situation.

Robert Mitchum and Janet Leigh in *Holiday Affair.* **She was not really old enough at age 22 to be the mom of a seven-year-old son, but who really cares?**

4. *River of No Return* - 1954

River of No Return is a pretty good Western, but the key is the pairing of Mitchum and Marilyn Monroe. This time, he's the one with the young son, and she is a saloon singer in the Old West who is the girlfriend of bad guy Rory Calhoun.

Set in the Northwest in 1875, *River* centers around Matt Calder (Robert Mitchum), an ex-convict and widower who is basically a recluse who lives on a remote farm with his young son Mark (Tommy Rettig). Matt helps two unexpected visitors who lose control of their raft on the nearby river. The man - Harry Weston (Rory Calhoun) - is a gambler by profession and he is racing to the nearest town to register a mining claim he has won in a poker game. His attractive wife Kay (Marilyn Monroe), a former saloon hall girl, is with him. When Calder refuses to let Weston have his only rifle and horse, he simply knocks Matt out, takes them, and leaves his wife behind. Unable to defend themselves against a likely Indian attack because Weston has stolen Matt's only means of defense, the three of them head for civilization.

Calder, his son, and Kay Weston begin the treacherous journey down the river on the raft Weston left behind. During the trip to Council City - where Weston is headed - they encounter rapids, a mountain lion, unfriendly Indians, and two gold prospectors who want to get rid of Mitchum so they can have Marilyn Monroe for themselves. Can you blame them for that?

In addition to Mitchum and Monroe, the best aspect of this film is the beautiful on-location color photography. *River* was filmed in Banff and Jasper national parks in Canada, as well as Lake Louise in Canada. The river was the Salmon River in Idaho.

Otto Preminger, who directed the film, had to contend with Mitchum's rather heavy drinking, but found Monroe extremely difficult to work with; Marilyn brought her own acting coach, Natasha Lytess, who constantly gave Monroe different directions from what Preminger gave her - never a good thing. The director really enjoyed working with the 12-year-old Rettig, who was very cooperative and actually bonded nicely with Monroe.

Overall the film featured a good plot, enough action sequences to make it interesting, and beautiful scenery photographed in CinemaScope. While not a great film, or even a great western, it has enough going for it to make this list of my favorite Mitchum films. Plus, anything with Marilyn Monroe in it always gets my attention!

If you remember Tommy Rettig, it is probably not for this film but for his most famous role - as Jeff Miller in the television series *Lassie* from 1954 to 1957.

Tommy Rettig and his pal, Lassie the dog, in the famous TV show *Lassie*.

5. *El Dorado* - 1967

Another good Robert Mitchum western, *El Dorado* is basically a remake of the earlier *Rio Bravo*, with John Wayne again playing the John Wayne part and Robert Mitchum playing the part of the drunken sheriff that Dean Martin played in the earlier film.

Hired gunman Cole Thornton (John Wayne) turns down a job with Bart Jason (Ed Asner) as it would mean having to fight an old sheriff friend, J.P. Harrah (Robert Mitchum). Some months later he finds out the lawman is generally drunk and a top gunfighter (Christopher George) is heading his way to help Jason. Along with an old Indian fighter (Arthur Hunnicutt instead of Walter Brennan) and young

Mississippi (a young James Caan instead of Ricky Nelson), handy with a knife who is also armed with a diabolical shotgun, Cole returns to help.

Wayne and Mitchum worked well together, and the film was directed by Howard Hawks, who also directed *Rio Bravo*. Hawks is right up there as one of the best directors of this era, with credits like *Red River*, *Sergeant York*, *The Big Sleep*, and *To Have and Have Not*.

> The latter two films starred Humphrey Bogart and Lauren Bacall.

6. *Cape Fear* - 1962

Another film where Robert Mitchum played a psychopath murderer with great effectiveness. This time he menaces Gregory Peck and his family.

Small-town Southern lawyer Sam Bowden (Gregory Peck)'s life becomes nightmarish when Max Cady (Robert Mitchum) re-enters his life. Cady went to jail for eight years after Bowden testified that Cady raped a young woman. Now that Cady has been released, he seeks his revenge by terrorizing Bowden and his family, particularly targeting Bowden's daughter, Nancy. Initially, Cady uses his newfound knowledge of the law (learned in prison) to annoy the Bowdens, then poisons the family dog. He then brutalizes a promiscuous woman. But the local sheriff (Martin Balsam) cannot prove that Cady killed the dog, and the woman is so afraid of Cady that she will not testify against him and instead leaves town.

Bowden moves his family to their houseboat, but will that be enough to stop Cady?

Mitchum delivers a performance that is menacing and reminds one of his earlier film, *Night of the Hunter*. He is scary because he is intelligent and unemotional in the pursuit of Peck and his family and seems to have acquired a law school education in his eight years in prison. Critics liked the film but censors were mixed on the extremely adult content of the film, especially for 1962. By the way, "Cape Fear" is a reference to the location of Bowden's houseboat. The film also stars Polly Bergen as Bowden's wife and Telly Savalas as the private investigator Bowden hires to keep an eye on Cady.

7. *Angel Face* - 1953

Generally Robert Mitchum's character is the scheming one but in this case he gets one-upped by Jean Simmons in this good film noir. This is another good Mitchum film directed by Otto Preminger.[35]

When Catherine Tremayne is mysteriously poisoned, ambulance driver Frank Jessup (Robert Mitchum) meets her refined but sensuous stepdaughter Diane (Jean Simmons), who quickly pursues and infatuates him. Under Diane's seductive influence, Frank is soon no longer an ambulance driver but the Tremayne chauffeur; but he begins to suspect danger under her surface sweetness. When he shows signs of pulling away, Diane schemes to get him in so deep he'll never get out. She manages to:

a. Alienate him from his girlfriend, played by Mona Freeman, who really loves him
b. Cook up a scheme where her mother may invest in Frank's desire to open up his own garage for automobile repairs; and.
c. Completely convince her father (Herbert Marshall) that she is a wonderful daughter, when she is actually a psycho and may be a murderer.
d. Keep Robert Mitchum baffled, quite a trick for an actor who is usually two steps ahead of everyone else in his films.

An excellent supporting cast includes Barbara O'Neill as Diane's mother, Leon Ames as the defense attorney, and Jim Backus (the voice of Mr. Magoo) as the prosecuting attorney.

---

35 In truth, it's probably better than *River of No Return*, since westerns were not really Otto Preminger's best genre by a longshot.

If you think you recognize Barbara O'Neill but can't place her, you are probably correct. She played Scarlett O'Hara's mother in *Gone with the Wind*.

Angel Face was the first American film for Jean Simmons. She was brought to the U.S. by Howard Hughes but managed to spurn his romantic advances. As a result, he refused to give her good parts, including *Roman Holiday*, which made a star out of Audrey Hepburn.

Robert Mitchum was certainly a different kind of leading man than actors like John Wayne, James Stewart, or Henry Fonda. And he was probably perfect for the more cynical times that began after the end of World War II.

6. Claudette Colbert (1903-1996)

Claudette Colbert was a major star in the 1930s and early 40s and continued her career on stage and on television. She was a very versatile actress who excelled in comedies as well as dramas. Of course, she will always be best known for her Oscar-winning role in *It Happened One Night*, a 1934 classic which won Academy Awards for Colbert as Best Actress and Clark Gable as best actor as well as Best Picture.

Biography

Born Lily Claudette Chauchoin in Paris in (1903), Claudette Colbert came to America as a child with her parents and studied art at the Art Students League. While there she became enthralled by the theatre. Without studying acting, she made her Broadway debut in 1923 in a minor play called "The Wild Wescotts." In a few years, Colbert was appearing in hit plays like "A Kiss in the Taxi" (1925) and the 1927 hit, "The Barker" with Walter Huston and Norman Foster, whom she married in 1928. "The Barker," in which she played a snake tamer, ran at Broadway's Biltmore Theatre, where she also later appeared in "Tin Pan Alley" in 1928 with Foster, whom she divorced in 1935; "The Kingfisher" with Rex Harrison in 1978; and "A Talent for Murder" with Jean-Pierre Aumont (1981).

Her other Broadway hits included "The Marriage-Go-Round" with Charles Boyer (1958) and her last New York appearance with Rex Harrison in "Aren't We All?" (1985).

Colbert's spectacular screen career began in 1927 and gathered steam with Ernest Lubitsch's *The Smiling Lieutenant* (1931) and Cecil B. DeMille's *The Sign of the Cross*, in which she played Nero's lascivious empress who bathed in donkeys' milk.

Her greatest triumph, however, was in Frank Capra's celebrated screwball comedy, *It Happened One Night* (1934), which neither she nor Clark Gable wanted to make. The film won five Academy Awards, including Oscars for her and Gable as well as Best Picture and Best Director (Frank Capra)[36] The movie established Colbert's resume as a star of both dramas and comedies. Other lighter films she made during the 1930s included *The Gilded Lily* (1935), *Tovarich* (1937), *Bluebeard's Eighth Wife* (1938), *Midnight* (1939) and *The Palm Beach Story* (1942).

She also proved her dramatic abilities in films like *Imitation of Life* (1934), *Cleopatra* (1934), *Drums Along the Mohawk* (1939) and on TV in *The Two Mrs. Grenvilles* (1986).

With her round face, big eyes, charming aristocratic manner, and flair for light comedy as well as drama, Colbert was known for a versatility that led to her becoming one of the best-paid stars of the 1930s and 1940s[37]. During her career, Colbert starred in more than sixty movies. She was the industry's highest-paid star in 1938 and 1942. Among her frequent co-stars were Fred MacMurray in seven films (1935–49), and Fredric March in four films (1930–33).

---

36 In other words, all four major awards

37 Colbert was a multi-millionaire at the time of her death

By the early 1950s, Colbert had basically retired from the screen in favor of television and stage work, and she earned a Tony Award nomination for *The Marriage-Go-Round* in 1959. Her career tapered off during the early 1960s, but in the late 1970s she experienced a career resurgence in theater, earning a Sarah Siddons Award for her Chicago theater work in 1980. For her television work in *The Two Mrs. Grenvilles* (1987) she won a Golden Globe Award and received an Emmy Award nomination.

Claudette Colbert was married twice. Her first husband was director/actor/writer Norman Foster, whom she married in 1928 and divorced in 1935. That same year Colbert married her second husband, Dr. Joel Pressman. He died in 1968.

Claudette Colbert died in 1996 as the age of 92. In 1999, the American Film Institute posthumously voted Colbert the 12th Greatest Female star of classic Hollywood cinema.

Awards

Claudette Colbert won a Best Actress Oscar for the 1934 film, *It Happened One Night*. She was also nominated for Best Actress for the 1935 film, *Private Lives*, as well as for the 1944 film, *Since You Went Away*.

Colbert won an Emmy for the 1987 television production, *The Two Mrs. Grenvilles*, and also a Golden Globe award for the same made-for-television film.

My Favorite Claudette Colbert Films

I have included a mix of comedies and dramas, which is certainly appropriate for her.

1. *It Happened One Night* - 1934
2. *The Palm Beach Story* - 1942
3. *Since You Went Away* - 1944
4. *So Proudly We Hail* - 1943
5. *Drums Along the Mohawk* - 1939
6. *The Egg and I* - 1947

1. *It Happened One Night* - 1934

This outstanding 1934 film became the prototype of the sophisticated romantic comedy, which led to films like *The Philadelphia Story, My Man Godfrey, Bringing Up Baby, You Can't Take it With You, The Lady Eve,* and *His Girl Friday,* among others, including a bunch of films with Spencer Tracy and Katharine Hepburn. And the two most famous scenes - Claudette Colbert's successful attempt to flag down a car while they were hitchhiking - where the street-smart Clark Gable had failed - and the famous Wall of Jericho scene in the hotel room - are among the most famous and respected scenes in American films.[38]

Spoiled heiress Ellen "Ellie" Andrews (Claudette Colbert) has eloped with pilot and fortune-hunter King Westley against the wishes of her extremely wealthy father, Alexander Andrews. Andrews wants to have the marriage annulled because he knows Westley is really only interested in her money, and he is right about that. Jumping ship in Florida, Ellie runs away and boards a Greyhound bus to New York City to reunite with her husband. She meets fellow bus passenger Peter Warne, a freshly out-of-work newspaper reporter who desperately needs a story. Soon Warne recognizes her and gives her a choice: If she will give him an exclusive on her story, he will help her reunite with Westley. If not, he will tell her father where she is. Ellie agrees to the first choice.

While at first, they show extreme dislike for one another, that eventually changes - of course, this is a romantic comedy! But not before several obstacles come into play.

It Happened One Night was the first film to win the Oscar in all five major categories - Best Picture, Best Actor (Gable), Best Actress (Colbert), Best Director (Frank Capra), and Best Writer (Robert Riskin).

While the supporting cast is good, the two leads are the centerpiece of the film, and they are brilliant. Gable has never been wittier, and

---

38 Apparently, Clark Gable's undressing with him not wearing an undershirt resulted in a dramatic drop in the sale of men's undershirts, the first case of a movie having an effect on a product.

Colbert is amazing as the spoiled heiress who is very human and very appealing at the same time. *It Happened One Night* always makes the list of the best American films of all time, and rightly so.

Claudette Colbert and Clark Gable in the famous Walls of Jericho scene from *It Happened One Night*. Frank Capra came up with the idea because Claudette Colbert refused to undress in front of the camera.

Frank Capra was simply one of the best directors in the history of American films. In addition to this film, Capra won Oscars for *You Can't Take It With You* and *Mr. Deeds Goes to Town*. Born in Sicily, Capra came to America at age 6. He was nominated for Best Director for three other films, including *Mr. Smith Goes to Washington*, and the classic holiday film, *It's a Wonderful Life*. Graduating with a degree from Cal Tech, Capra started in the motion picture business as an extra and prop man and eventually became a director.

2. *The Palm Beach Story* - 1942

The Palm Beach Story is a good screwball comedy[39], with fast pacing and snappy dialogue featuring Claudette Colbert and the under-rated Joel McCrea.

Gerry and Tom Jeffers (Claudette Colbert and Joel McCrea, also included in this book) - are finding married life to be financially hard. Tom is an inventor/architect and there is little money for them to live on. They are about to be thrown out of their apartment when Gerry meets a rich businessman being shown around as a prospective tenant. He gives Gerry $700 to start life afresh but Tom refuses to believe her story and they quarrel. Gerry decides the marriage is over and heads to Palm Beach for a quick divorce but Tom has plans to stop her. A series of challenges takes place in this very funny comedy.

Directed by Preston Sturges and co-starring Mary Astor and Rudy Vallee, one of the highlights of the film is when Colbert encounters the drunken members of the Ale and Quail Club, a group of hunters whose actions cry out for more gun control. That is all I will say about that scene.

3. *Since You Went Away* - 1944

Since You Went Away is another excellent World War II film, but in this case about the people left behind by the soldiers who fought the war in Europe and Asia.

While husband Tim is away during World War II, Anne Hilton (Claudette Colbert) copes with more normal, everyday problems at home. Taking in a lodger, Colonel Smollett (Monty Wooley), to help make ends meet, and dealing with shortages and rationing are minor inconveniences compared to the love affair between her daughter Jane (Jennifer Jones) and the Colonel's grandson (Robert Walker).

---

39 A form of comedy film that thrived in the 1940s and featured a smart female who is very much the match for her male counterpart and results in a battle of the sexes. Spencer Tracy and Katharine Hepburn made several of them.

Since You Went Away is both a sentimental and realistic World War II movie. The film is set in a mid-sized American town, where people with loved ones in the Armed Forces try to cope with their changed circumstances and make their own contributions to the war effort. Anne volunteers at a local military hospital, for example.

Although generally positive, *Since You Went Away* is somber at times about the effects of war on ordinary people. Some characters on the home front are dealing with grief, loneliness, or fear for their futures. Wounded and disabled troops are shown in the hospital scenes. It has a great cast, which also includes Joseph Cotten, Lionel Barrymore, Agnes Moorehead, Hattie McDaniel, and Shirley Temple. The film won an Oscar for Max Steiner for Best Musical Score and was nominated for eight other Oscars, including Jennifer Jones for Best Supporting Actress.[40]

The film was a huge success, earning almost $5 million in ticket sales - quite a nice sum in those days.

> Robert Walker's life is quite a sad story. He was a very young and promising actor (only 25 when this film was made), but he never recovered from his divorce from Jennifer Jones. He died in 1951 from a combination of alcohol and barbiturates at the age of 32. By far his best film was his terrific performance as the psychotic killer in Alfred Hitchcock's *Strangers on a Train*, with Farley Granger and Walker in equal starring roles. Walker's son, Robert Walker, Jr. is also an actor.

40　At the time, Jennifer Jones and Robert Walker were married in real life but were going through a bitter divorce. She was having an affair with the film's producer, David O. Selznick, her eventual husband.

In *Strangers on a Train,* Farley Granger (left) and Robert Walker are strangers who discuss the possibility of murdering someone that each of them hates - Granger's miserable wife and Walker's father. Actually, Walker does the proposing and Granger listens in utter disbelief. And where does this discussion take place? On a train, of course.

4. *So Proudly We Hail* - 1944

This wonderful World War II film shows the war from the point of view of the nurses who served during WWII.

A group of U.S. Army nurses - including Claudette Colbert, Paulette Goddard, Veronica Lake, and Barbara Britton - leave San Francisco for their tour of duty in Hawaii in December 1941. The attack on Pearl Harbor changes their destination, and their lives. Sent to Bataan, in the Philippines, the nurses are led by Lt. Janet Davidson (Colbert). She is faced with untested nurses who expected an easy time in Honolulu, but who quickly become battle-weary veterans dealing with daily bombardments by the Japanese, overwhelmed by the numbers of wounded, and dwindling supplies. Some of Davidson's unit also have to deal with romantic entanglements with men they met onboard ship, including future television Superman George Reeves. When Bataan falls, the American forces flee to the offshore island of Corregidor, where they find the Japanese assault just as intense.

This movie was perhaps the only World War II film shown from the point of view of the women directly involved in the war, and was a very inspirational effort. Filmed just after the Japanese attack on Bataan and Corregidor, that fact was fresh on the minds of American filmgoers viewing this film.

So Proudly We Hail was nominated for four Oscars, including Paulette Goddard for Best Supporting Actress. Goddard is breathtakingly beautiful in her films, and generally gave a good performance. She lost out to Vivien Leigh in *Gone with the Wind* but starred in one of my favorite films, *Reap the Wild Wind*, with John Wayne and Ray Milland. She was also married - we think! - to Charley Chaplin.

Paulette Goddard as one of the nurses in *So Proudly We Hail*.

5. *Drums Along the Mohawk* - 1939

Drums Along the Mohawk is a very good "Western" if you can call a film that takes place in upstate New York a western.

In Revolutionary War rural America, Gil Martin (Henry Fonda) takes his new wife Lana (Claudette Colbert) back to his farm in upstate New York. The area is remote and a distance from the fort but they are happy living in their one room cabin.

With the declaration of independence, however, the settlers soon find themselves at war with both the British and their Native American allies. Their farm is burned out and the Martins move in with Sarah McKlennar (the always good Edna Mae Oliver).[41] The war continues, however, as the Martins try to make a new life. When they are attacked by the Indians, their only hope for survival is for Gil to run to the fort without being caught by the warriors in what seems to be about a ten mile run.

Directed brilliantly by John Ford, the movie paints a beautiful picture of early America from the point of view of people living away from the main cities. The film was nominated for two Oscars, one for Best Cinematography and one for Best Supporting Actress (Edna Mae Oliver, of course). While the film took place in upstate New York, it was actually filmed in a remote part of Idaho. *Drums* also starred Ward Bond and John Carradine among others.

> Henry Fonda had a special connection to *Drums*. The Fondas were originally Dutch settlers who settled in upstate New York.

---

41 If I ever do a book about great American supporting actors of the 30s, 40s, and 50s, Edna Mae Oliver is a must. Among her most famous roles was that of Lady Catherine de Bourgh in the 1940 version of *Pride and Prejudice* with Greer Garson and Laurence Olivier. And I can't forget her as Miss Pross in the 1935 version of *A Tale of Two Cities* with Ronald Colman.

Is that an American revolutionary war soldier? No, it's Edna Mae Oliver defending her home in *Drums Along the Mohawk*, with Henry Fonda and Claudette Colbert.

6. *The Egg and I* - 1947

Long before he played Steve Douglas in the television hit *My Three Sons*, Fred MacMurray was a bit hit on the big screen in comedies, westerns and even dramatic roles like *Double Indemnity*.

The Egg and I is based on a best-selling book by Betty Macdonald that tells the story of life on a farm as an adult, with no experience in farming. On their wedding night Bob MacDonald (Fred MacMurray) informs his new bride Betty (Claudette Colbert) that he has bought a chicken farm. An abandoned chicken farm, to be exact, which is obvious when the two move in. Their trials and tribulations are amusing and realistic. Betty endures Bob's enthusiasm for the rural life, rustic inconveniences, and battling nature, but her patience is severely tested when glamorous neighbor Harriet Putnam (Louise Allbritton) seems to set her sights on Bob. As it happens, Harriet owns a very modern farm down the road, replete with farmhands, technology, conveniences, but "no Man."

This very funny comedy marked the first screen appearance of Ma and Pa Kettle (Marjorie Main and Percy Kilbride), who owned a nearby farm and had 15 children; Ma and Pa Kettle had their series of nine movies between 1949 and 1956, the last two of which were filmed without Kilbride.

The Egg and I was nominated for one Oscar, Marjorie Main for Best Supporting Actress - not surprising, since she was very good in the role.

Marjorie Main (Ma Kettle) introducing Claudette Colbert (Betty MacDonald) to farm life in *The Egg and I.*

Claudette Colbert was everything one could ask for in a movie star - good at both comedy and drama, and a good enough actress to win an Oscar for *It Happened One Night*. She was also one of those rare movie stars who was able to move into theater and television later in her career without missing a beat.

7. Van Heflin (1908-1971)

Van Heflin was an extremely versatile actor who shifted between hero and villain and between leading man and supporting actor with equal ease. Certainly not the handsomest actor to ever grace the silver screen, he made up for it by being very hard working and a really good actor. Of his 67 movie and television roles - mostly in films - several really stand out, including his Oscar-winning performance in the 1941 crime drama, *Johnny Eager*.[42]

Biography

Van Heflin was born Emmett Evan Heflin in Walters, Oklahoma in December 1908, the son of Fanny Bleecker (Shippey) and Emmett Evan Heflin, a dental surgeon. When his parents separated, his brother and sister stayed with his mother, while he was sent to live with his grandmother in California. He never quite settled in there, and his restless spirit led him to ship out on a tramp steamer after graduating from school. After a year at sea he studied for a law degree at the

---

42   Robert Taylor, not Van Heflin, played the title character.

University of Oklahoma, but after two years he decided he had enough and went back to sailing the Pacific. When he returned to land, he decided to try his hand at acting and enrolled at the prestigious Yale School of Drama. His first foray into theatre was the comedy "Mister Moneypenny"[43] (1928) (credited as "Evan Heflin"). It was indifferently received and Van went back to sea, this time for three years. In 1934 he returned to the stage in the plays "The Bride of Torozko" and "The Night Remembers," both outright disasters. During this period he also earned a bachelor's degree from the University of Oklahoma and a master's degree in theater from Yale University.

After all this unsettled experience, Van Heflin's big break came in 1936, when he landed a good leading role as a radical leftist at odds with the established elite in the S.N. Behrman comedy of manners, "End of Summer" at the Guild Theatre. Katharine Hepburn, who saw him on stage in this play, then persuaded Van to try film acting and finagled a role for him alongside her in the Pandro S. Berman production *A Woman Rebels* (1936). Van spent a year at RKO in forgettable films, with roles ranging from a reverend in *The Outcasts of Poker Flat* (1937) to a top-billed part as a burnt-out quarterback who sounds off against the politics involved in college football in *Saturday's Heroes* (1937). But he was back on Broadway in a very successful run of "The Philadelphia Story" in 1939.

On the strength of these performances, Van was signed to a contract at MGM, where he remained for eight years (1941-49). His tenure was interrupted only by two years of wartime service as a combat photographer with the U.S. 9th Air Force, First Motion Picture Unit, which produced training and morale-boosting short films. Back at MGM, his third assignment at the studio, *Johnny Eager* (1941), proved an excellent showcase for his acting skills. He played Jeff Hartnett, right-hand man of the titular crime figure (Robert Taylor), a complex, sardonic character, on one hand a loyal soldier yet tremendously self-loathing at the same time. For his role as the heavy-drinking, Shakespeare-quoting mobster with a conscience, Van got the Academy Award as Best Supporting Actor in 1943. He was immediately cast in the leading role as a forensically-minded detective in *Kid Glove*

---

43   I assume no relation to the James Bond character, Miss Moneypenny.

Killer (1942), a film which marked the debut of Fred Zinnemann as a feature director. This was in turn followed by another B-movie whodunit, *Grand Central Murder* (1942).

Over the next 20 years, Heflin enjoyed his greatest success in Hollywood, performing in such films as *Battle Cry*, *The Three Musketeers*, *Shane*, *The Strange Love of Martha Ivers*, and *3:10 to Yuma*, where he was equally good as heroes and heels. In addition, he alternated between westerns, costume dramas, war movies, and dramas without showing a weakness in any area.

Beginning in the 1960s, Heflin starred on Broadway and in Hollywood, playing in the hit stage production "A Case of Libel" and—in his last movie—played the World War II demolitions expert determined to blow up a plane in the box office smash *Airport*. The role was in many ways typically Van Heflin—though he often insisted there was no such thing. "I've never played the same part twice," he said once. "I'm a character actor, always have been."[44]

Nevertheless, he generally played a supporting character, seemingly hard-bitten, but possessed of a certain vulnerability beneath the rugged facade, a weakness that ultimately brought him to bad ends.

He was extremely easy to work with on screen, according to those he worked with. For example, Ross Hunter, his producer on *Airport* said: "I've never known a kinder, simpler, more understanding man. People didn't realize this—his talent overshadowed it all."[45]

Unlike many of his peers, Van shunned the limelight and was never a part of the Hollywood glamour set. A physical fitness fanatic throughout much of his career, Heflin was taking his daily 20 laps in the pool when he suffered a fatal heart attack at the age of 62.

Awards

Van Heflin won a Best Supporting Actor Oscar for his performance as a gangster with a conscience in 1943 for *Johnny Eager*. He was

---

44   International Movie Data Base article on Van Heflin

45   Ibid, also from Van Heflin's autobiography

nominated for an Emmy for Outstanding Performance by an Actor in a drama for *A Case of Libel* in 1968. He was nominated for the Best Foreign Actor by BAFTA[46] for *Shane* in 1954. Finally, He was nominated for a Golden Laurel award for Top Male Action Star for *3:10 to Yuma* in 1958 and ended up fourth. (One of my all-time favorite stars, Burt Lancaster, won for *Gunfight at the O.K. Corral.*)

My Favorite Van Heflin Films

I have listed dramas, westerns, a swashbuckler, and a war film among my favorite Van Heflin movies. All were made between 1940 and 1959.

1. *3:10 to Yuma* -1957
2. *Johnny Eager* - 1941
3. *Shane* - 1953
4. *The Strange Love of Martha Ivers* - 1946
5. *Battle Cry* - 1955
6. *Gunman's Walk* - 1958
7. *They Came to Cordura* - 1959
8. *The Three Musketeers* - 1948

1. *3:10 to Yuma* - 1957

Probably Van Heflin's best Western film, and actually superior to the 2007 Russell Crowe/Christian Bale version. And believe it or not, Van Heflin is the hero and Glenn Ford (almost always the hero in westerns) is the heavy.

From the opening scene of a stagecoach moving along the barren desert to the closing moment at the railroad station, this is simply an outstanding western with a good plot and great acting from the two leads.After notorious outlaw leader Ben Wade (Glenn Ford) is captured in a small western town, his gang continues to threaten. Small-time rancher Dan Evans (Van Heflin) is persuaded to take Wade in secret to the nearest town with a railway station to await the train to the court and prison in Yuma, and Wade's bunch vows that will never happen. Drought has threatened Evans' ranch, and he decides the only way he can keep the ranch going is to accept the $200 money offered by the stage coach line owner to take Ben Wade to that town. Once the two

---

46   BAFTA is the British version of the Academy Awards

are holed up in the hotel to wait the arrival of the train (at 3:10 of course), the rest of the party deserts, leaving Dan to get Ben Wade on that train while Wade's gang of seven attempts to prevent their leader from going to jail.

Heflin is extremely noble and a wonderful husband and father to his two sons, but his wife questions whether it is worth risking his life to make $200. However, it is Ford who really makes the film. He is so very charming and respectful of Dan and his wife (Leora Dana) that you almost forget that this fellow is a cold-blooded killer.[47]

Popular singer Frankie Laine sang the title song, and the supporting cast includes Felicia Farr, Richard Jaeckel as Wade's right-hand man, and Henry Jones.

Good guy Van Heflin (right) trying to get bad guy Glenn Ford to the railroad station in *3:10 to Yuma*.

2. *Johnny Eager - 1941*[48]

---

47 In the 2007 version, you never forget for one second that Russell Crowe is a vicious killer.

48 *Johnny Eager* was filmed in 1941 but did not debut until January 1942, making it eligible for the 1943 Oscars.

MGM - generally not noted for its crime movies - apparently decided they need to toughen up Robert Taylor's "pretty boy" image, so they cast him as a tough guy gang leader in this 1941 gangster flick.

Taylor plays a parolee who is pretending to follow the straight-and-narrow as a hardworking cabbie, but is really the mastermind behind a dog-racing track being built with mob money. Johnny Eager works every angle, has a gang that's generally in line, and also has a loyal right-hand man in Jeff Hartnett (Van Heflin), his educated assistant, who drinks too much and recites poetry when he isn't looking after Johnny's interests (and sometimes when he is, too). Eager has only one problem, special prosecutor John Benson Farrell (Edward Arnold) - who was also the attorney instrumental in sending Eager to prison - has gotten an injunction against the racetrack's opening. But Eager sees an opening when he accidentally crosses paths with a young sociology student, Lisbeth Bard (Lana Turner), who is drawn to him romantically, and then finds out that she's Farrell's step-daughter.

After romancing her for a few months, he sets her up in a scam, making her believe that she killed one of Eager's men (Paul Stewart in an unlikely role as a Hispanic). He "generously" gets her away from the scene and then informs Farrell of what has happened, pointing out that he holds the evidence against Lisbeth. Farrell has no choice but to withdraw the injunction, and the track opens, but problems ensue when rival mobsters decide to try and cut in on Eager and his racket, and he finds out that Lisbeth is so guilt-ridden over her "crime," that she's destroying herself mentally.

Eager can't figure out why she feels the way she does or what to do about it, or even if he should do anything to help her, but with Jeff's help, he discovers a nobler side to his nature. Realizing that she really does love him, and knowing it's not possible for the two of them to be together, he goes out in a blaze of glory - laced with a special irony built into the plot - solving Lisbeth's problem and also curing her of her love for him, and settling a score or two in the process.

Everything about *Johnny Eager* is first-rate, including the quality of stars and the acting, which puts it a cut above most film noir movies. Taylor, not the greatest actor in the world, is very good in the title role, and

Heflin's performance as the educated right-hand man is Oscar worthy. And Taylor and beautiful Lana Turner make a great-looking couple.

Handsome Robert Taylor and gorgeous Lana Turner in *Johnny Eager*

3. *Shane* - 1953

I have already covered *Shane* under the section on Alan Ladd. Let me add that Van Heflin co-stars as the steady and reliable homesteader Joe Starrett, who simply wants to have a place for he, his wife, and son to carve out a living. Heflin is no shrinking violet, but he is certainly not the man of action (or the man with a past) that Alan Ladd as Shane is. But the two make a very effective team in taking on the Rykers. And Heflin is good in contrasting his character with the more charismatic Shane, and we see the different strengths and weaknesses of the two men.

4. *The Strange Love of Martha Ivers* - 1946

I have said several times that Van Heflin alternated between playing the hero and the villain with equal ease. In *The Strange Love of Martha Ivers*, Heflin is the hero, Lizabeth Scott is the heroine, while Barbara Stanwyck and Kirk Douglas are the villains in this drama/film noir.

In 1928, young heiress Martha Ivers (Barbara Stanwyck in a menacing role that she plays so well) decides not to run off with friend Sam Masterson (Van Heflin), and instead is involved in a series of fatal events. Years later, Sam returns to the Pennsylvania town of Iverstown (get it?) to find Martha the power behind Iverstown and married to the generally drunk weakling Walter O'Neil (Kirk Douglas[49]), now district attorney. At first, Sam is more interested in displaced blonde Toni Marachek (Lizabeth Scott as the damsel in distress) than in his boyhood friends, but they draw him into a convoluted web of plotting and cross-purposes.

The performances are all good, especially Heflin and Stanwyck (always good). The film was nominated for only one Oscar, but this was the year (1947) that the Oscars were dominated by one of the great American films of all time, *The Best Years of Our Lives*.

Van Heflin befriending Lizabeth Scott in *The Strange Love of Martha Ivers*. I can certainly see why he would want to help her.

5. *Battle Cry* - 1955

---

49   This was the film debut of Issur Danielovitch, who we all know as Kirk Douglas. Douglas said that Heflin was extremely helpful to him on the set.

This solid 1955 war movie follows a group of WWII marines from basic training to the battlefield.. All this changes with an onslaught of heavy-duty battling in the South Pacific.

In 1942, a group of young men including Aldo Ray and Tab Hunter, join the Marines, leaving loved ones behind. Major Sam Huxley (Van Heflin) knows that his men are spoiling for a real fight but must make do with the small skirmishes assigned them for the time being. Primed for battle, they are frustrated by these non-combat assignments, as we follow their wartime romances, especially Andy Hookens' (Ray) involvement with Pat (Nancy Olson), a New Zealand widow. Andy and Pat have just decided that war requires them to "live for the moment" when, in 1944, the team finally goes into a real battle at Tarawa. A great cast also includes Dorothy Malone (more about her later), Raymond Massey, Mona Freeman, James Whitmore, and Anne Francis, among others. The real plus of *Battle Cry* is the way it explores the human elements of war.

The movie is based on the novel by former Marine Leon Uris, who also wrote the screenplay, and was produced and directed by Raoul Walsh. The film was shot at Camp Pendleton, California and featured a large amount of cooperation from the United States Marine Corps.

Aldo Ray is a very interesting story. An actual Navy frogman during World War II who saw action at Iwo Jimi, his gruff exterior, husky frame, and raspy voice - a frogman who sounded like a frog - allowed him to play a lot of tough-guy roles. This included the part of an escaped prisoner in *We're No Angels*, with Humphrey Bogart.

6. *Gunman's Walk* - 1958

I picked this 1958 western because of the conflict between father and sons, or at least a father and his elder son.

Widower Lee Hackett (Van Heflin), a cattle rancher who is a product of the old west, tries to bring up his two sons, Ed (Tab Hunter) and Davy (James Darren), in his image. While Davy is a decent fellow, Ed is wild, violent, and unruly. The two brothers are both attracted to Clee Chourard (Kathryn Grant)) but she prefers Davy. Ed's efforts to outshine his father and brother and everyone else around leads him into a career as a gunfighter, and leads to an eventual confrontation with his father.

An interesting film with an intriguing message. Heflin raises his eldest son without any discipline but prefers him over the younger son, who is viewed as weak because he is kinder and gentler. Heflin views his role as running roughshod over others as the way to get ahead but only too late realizes that he has transmitted these views to his older son. It is interesting to see the blond-haired, blue-eyed Tab Hunter play the villain instead of the hero.[50]

Matinee idol **Tab Hunter** in a scene from *Battle Cry*, the previous film.

---

50 I guess "Tab Hunter" sounded and looked a lot better on a marquee than his real name, Arthur Kelm.

7. *They Came to Cordura* - 1959

They Came to Cordura is a 1959 Gary Cooper western with a fine supporting cast. This was the last western that Cooper made in his wonderful career.[51]

After a cavalry charge during the 1916 U.S. "war against Pancho Villa," disgraced awards officer Tom Thorn (Gary Cooper) receives an assignment to find five men who should receive the U.S. Medal of Honor for gallantry and bravery in action. It is a cynical act by Washington, because 1) the purpose is purely public relations for a botched armed intervention; and 2) Cooper's Major Thorn is actually given the assignment because he behaved cowardly (supposedly) on the field of battle. For the Major to be given this quiet assignment is actually an insult - his own courage is being questioned.

Taking his five men with him (Richard Conte, Van Heflin, Michael Callan, Tab Hunter, and Dick York), Cooper starts trying to get to know them. He soon discovers that the men are not interested in the medal, and (as they have a long trek to Cordura, where they have to go to finalize the awards), Cooper learns that the men are not very noble at all. To worsen things, they capture an American hacienda owner (Rita Hayworth), who gave assistance to Villa's men. The woman reawakens sexual tensions and rivalries between the five men, as well as Cooper.[52]

Cooper plays his generally stalwart role as the officer, and the five "heroes" behave badly throughout the trip. The other supporting players, including Heflin as Sgt. John Chawk, are all given plenty of screen time. The movie's major weakness is that it is a bit talky with not enough action. Cooper was also much too old for the part he was playing and he was in poor health during the making of the film.

8. *The Three Musketeers* - 1948

---

51 Cooper passed away from prostate cancer the following year - 1960.

52 Not surprising - after all, it is Rita Hayworth!

The 1948 film version of the Alexandre Dumas novel is notable for two reasons - the great Gene Kelly as D'Artagnan, and Van Heflin as the leader of the musketeers, Athos. As a huge fan of swashbucklers, I found the swordfighting choreography to be spectacular.[53]

The film follows the general content of the Dumas novel. The young Gascon D'Artagnan travels to Paris to join the King's Musketeers but is robbed and beaten along the way. In Paris he spots one of his assailants and in his haste to confront him, annoys three of the most skillful Musketeers: Athos (Van Heflin), Porthos (Gig Young) and Aramis (Robert Coote). Each challenges him to a duel. At the appointed place, upon learning they are all there to duel the same man, the master swordsmen are amused by the newcomer's audacity.

Before they can begin, however, they are interrupted by Cardinal Richelieu's (Vincent Price's) guards, who try to arrest the Musketeers. Outraged that the three are outnumbered, D'Artagnan joins them in dispatching their foes, displaying his superb swordsmanship in the process. As a result, he is welcomed into their ranks. Of course, a series of adventures follows, including trouble between England and France, and D'Artagnan draws the attention of two women - one good, Constance (June Allyson) and one bad (Milady, Countess de Winter, played by Lana Turner).

The Three Musketeers was one of the most popular films of 1948 and grossed over $4 million, a nice sum for the time. It was nominated for an Oscar for Best Color Cinematography but lost out to *Joan of Arc*.

As I hope I have demonstrated, Van Heflin was an outstanding actor who could play a variety of roles in westerns, dramas, film noir, and even swashbucklers. He could be the hero or the heel and he was equally good as the lead or a supporting actor. He truly deserves to be a star worth remembering.

---

53 Of course, any film starring Gene Kelly is bound to have outstanding choreography.

8. Ava Gardner (1922-1990)

Ava Gardner was one of the most beautiful actresses in the history of film, and not a bad actress either, when she got the chance to act. A small town girl from the rural South, Ava Lavina Gardner became one of Hollywood's biggest stars of the late 1940s and 1950s. She had three famous marriages - to Mickey Rooney (believe it or not), bandleader Artie Shaw, and Frank Sinatra, who considered Ava Gardner the love of his life - and why not? Ava Gardner is consistently ranked among the most beautiful movie stars of all time.

Biography

Ava Lavina Gardner was born in Grabtown, North Carolina, on December 24, 1922. She was her parents' seventh child. When Gardner was two years old, she and her family were forced to leave their tobacco farm. Her father then worked as a sharecropper, while her mother ran a boardinghouse. The family always struggled financially, a situation that worsened when Gardner's father died when she was 16.

Ava Gardner was studying to be a secretary when her photographer brother-in-law sent pictures of her to Metro-Goldwyn-Mayer. A striking beauty with dark hair and green eyes, Gardner's photos convinced the studio to give her a screen test. This led to her signing a seven-year, $50/week contract with MGM in 1941, when Gardner was 18 years old.

Upon her arrival in Hollywood, Ava Gardner was put into the MGM studio system to learn how to be an actress. Her thick Southern accent made speech lessons a required part of her training. Gardner was shy and intimidated by the process of appearing on camera, and would sometimes drink beforehand to calm her nerves.

Limited to bit parts at first, Gardner slowly worked her way up to larger roles. But it wasn't until she was loaned to Universal Studios to appear as seductress Kitty Collins in 1946's *The Killers* that Gardner became a star. That success led to the actress landing better parts in movies like *The Hucksters* (1947), *Show Boat* (1951) and *The Snows of Kilimanjaro* (1952). She also appeared in *Mogambo* (1953), a role that paired her with Clark Gable and earned Gardner her only Academy Award nomination.

Even though her acting abilities improved with time, Gardner's beauty was always a large part of her appeal. For her role in *The Barefoot Contessa* (1954), as a dancer whose rags-to-riches story echoed Gardner's own, MGM touted her as "The World's Most Beautiful Animal."

Ava Gardner's life in Hollywood was also busy off camera. She met actor Mickey Rooney on her first studio visit in California. Rooney, then at the height of his career, ardently pursued her. As Gardner, heeding her North Carolina upbringing, was determined to remain a virgin until marriage, they wed in 1942, after first receiving permission from MGM. The two separated a year later, amid Gardner's accusations that Rooney had been unfaithful. (Was he crazy?)

With the end of her first marriage, the down-to-earth Gardner's reputation for drinking, smoking, and partying grew. She also became close with playboy Howard Hughes. Although Gardner refused to have an affair with Hughes, she remained an object of fascination for the reclusive man for years. Gardner had another short marriage, from 1945 to 1946, to bandleader Artie Shaw. During their time together, Shaw tried to mold Gardner, who was already insecure about her lack of education, with suggested reading lists.

Gardner rarely shied away from romantic entanglements, and her partners ranged from co-stars to Spanish matadors. Her real-life femme fatale reputation peaked when she became involved with singer Frank Sinatra, whom she also considered the love of her life. After Sinatra left his wife to be with Gardner, the two married in 1951. Unfortunately, their passion often boiled over into jealous fights, and the two separated and reconciled several times before finally divorcing in 1957.

Gardner left her MGM contract in 1958, but continued to appear in movies, including *On the Beach* (1959) and *The Night of the Iguana* (1964). Now in her 40s, Gardner received fewer job offers as the years passed, working only sporadically.

After living in Spain for several years, Gardner moved to London, England, in 1968. She remained close to Sinatra, who called her hospital room after her 1986 stroke and later helped with her medical bills. Ava Gardner died from pneumonia in London on January 25, 1990, at the age of 67. She was buried next to her parents in North Carolina.

Awards
Ava Gardner was nominated for a Best Actress Oscar in 1954 for *Mogambo* but lost out to Audrey Hepburn in *Roman Holiday*. She was nominated for a Golden Globe award in 1965 for *Night of the Iguana* and was nominated for three BAFTA awards for *Bhowani Junction*, *On the Beach*, and *The Night of the Iguana*, but did not win either of those awards.

My Favorite Ava Gardner Movies
1. *The Killers* - 1946

2. *On the Beach* - 1959
3. *Show Boat* - 1951
4. *Mogambo* - 1953
5. *Seven Days in May* - 1964
6. *The Snows of Kilimanjaro* - 1952

1. *The Killers* - 1946

The Killers was the first movie role for Burt Lancaster and the first starring role for Ava Gardner, and they were terrific together. The film begins with two professional killers (William Conrad and Charles McGraw) entering a small town and killing a gas station attendant, ex-boxer "the Swede," (Burt Lancaster) who's expecting them. The rest of the movie is a series of flashbacks as insurance investigator Jim Reardon (Edmond O'Brien) pursues the case against the orders of his boss, who considers it trivial, based on the small amount of the Swede's insurance policy - $2,500. Weaving together threads of the Swede's life, Reardon uncovers a complex tale of treachery, double crossing, and crime, all linked with gorgeous, mysterious Kitty Collins (Ava Gardner).

As Reardon investigates the killing, he encounters characters such as police lieutenant Sam Lubinsky (Sam Levene), the Swede's former pal until the latter turned to a life of crime; and gang leader Big Jim Colfax (Albert Dekker), the other man in Ava Gardner's life. But it is the chemistry between Lancaster and Gardner that really makes this noir film special, and catapulted their characters.

My two favorite male movie stars have always been John Wayne and Burt Lancaster. In just about all of Lancaster's films, including this one, his charisma explodes off the screen. Lancaster won a Best Actor Oscar for *Elmer Gantry* in 1961 but easily could have won a few more, including *From Here to Eternity* and *The Birdman of Alcatraz*.

Burt Lancaster and Ava Gardner in *The Killers*

2. *On the Beach* - 1959

Directed by the great Stanley Kramer, this depressing but well-acted film featured Gregory Peck and Ava Gardner in starring roles. In 1964, atomic war wipes out humanity in the northern hemisphere and leaves the rest of the world facing extinction from nuclear fallout. One American submarine finds a temporary safe haven in Australia (which is just about all that is left of humanity), where life-as-usual masks a growing concern. In the midst of this, and with children back in San Francisco, American Captain Dwight Towers (Gregory Peck) meets survivor Moira Davidson (Ava Gardner), who begins to fall for him. The sub sets out for home, but after reconnaissance they find there is no one left alive on the West Coast. So will Towers and Moira find comfort with each other before the inevitable unhappy conclusion?

On the Beach was filmed on location in and near Melbourne, Australia. It received excellent reviews but lost $700,000 at the box office, probably because of its very depressing theme - the likely end of the world. But the movie is probably more relevant today than ever before, with the possibility of the end of the world because of nuclear attack even more probable than ever.

An excellent supporting cast includes Fred Astaire as a scientist and Anthony Perkins as a Navy officer. It was nominated for two Academy Awards for Best Film Editing and Best Musical Score but did not win in either category.

3. *Show Boat* - 1951

I have always been a big fan of movie musicals, and this version of the classic Broadway show written by Jerome Kern and Oscar Hammerstein II is one of the best.

The "Cotton Blossom", owned by the Hawks family (Joe E. Brown and Agnes Moorehead), is the show boat where everyone comes for great musical entertainment down South as the boat makes its way down the Mississippi River in the late 1800s and early 1900s. Julie LaVerne (Ava Gardner) and her husband (Robert Sterling) are the stars of the show. After a snitch on board tells the local police that Julie (who's half African-American) is married to a white man, the two stars are forced to leave the show boat. The reason being, that down South interracial marriages are forbidden.[54]

Magnolia Hawks (Kathryn Grayson), Captain Andy Hawks' daughter, becomes the new show boat attraction and her leading man is Gaylord Ravenal (Howard Keel), a gambler. The two instantly fall in love and marry, without her mother's approval. Magnolia and Gaylord leave the "Cotton Blossom" for a whirl-wind honeymoon and to live in a fantasy world - actually, Chicago. Magnolia soon faces reality quickly, that gambling means more to Gaylord than anything else. Magnolia confronts Gaylord, and after he gambles away their fortune he leaves her - not knowing she is pregnant. Magnolia is left penniless and pregnant, and is left to fend for herself. While we never see any more of Julie's husband, Julie appears at key occasions to attempt to bring the couple back together.

Kathryn Grayson and Howard Keel are as always an outstanding team - both of them are featured in my first book - but it is really the performance of Ava Gardner that steals the show. As the unfortunate Julie, her life quickly goes downhill when she leaves the show, and Ava Gardner's performance reflects how far she has fallen. She makes a desperate attempt to reunite Magnolia and Gaylord so they do not end up like her, and the final scene is brilliantly photographed. Plus, with songs like "Ol' Man River,""Make Believe,""Bill," and "Can't Help Lovin' Dat Man," how could you go wrong? No expense was spared in

54 Remember, this is the South, only 20 or so years after the end of the Civil War.

the production of this film, including constructing a river boat to serve as the Cotton Blossom. And while Ava Gardner reportedly had a beautiful singing voice, for some reason her singing was dubbed by popular singer Annette Warren.[55]

Others in the cast include the dancing team of Marge and Gower Champion and William Warfield, who sings "Ol' Man River" beautifully.

Kathryn Grayson and Howard Keel in *Show Boat*. They also starred together in the wonderful *Kiss Me Kate*.

4. *Mogambo* - 1953

Mogambo is essentially a remake of the 1932 Clark Gable hit *Red Dust*, with Ava Gardner and Grace Kelly substituting for Jean Harlow and Mary Astor in the original film.

Victor Marswell (Clark Gable) runs a big game trapping company in Kenya. Eloise Kelly (Ava Gardner) is stranded there, and an immediate attraction takes place between them. Then Mr. and Mrs. Nordley (Grace Kelly) show up for a gorilla documenting safari in the jungle. Mrs. Nordley is clearly not in love with her husband any more, and

---

55 As of the writing of this book, Annette Warren is 96 and still occasionally performing at clubs in the Los Angeles area. Wow!

takes a liking to Marswell. Scorned by Victor, Kelly tries to kill him, but true-blue Eloise takes the blame for the shooting.

Reportedly, Grace Kelly carried on an off-camera romance with Clark Gable, which ended when the differences in their ages (52 and 24) proved insurmountable. Even so, it is the easy rapport between Gable and Ava Gardner, in another strong performance, which stands out in *Mogambo*.

5. *Seven Days in May* -1964

This film, made later in her career when she was 42 and playing more character parts, is the only Ava Gardner movie from the 1960s that I have included.

An unpopular U.S. President (Fredric March) who is perceived as "soft" on communism, especially by the military, manages to get a nuclear disarmament treaty through the Senate, but finds that the nation is turning against him. Jiggs Casey (Kirk Douglas), a Marine Colonel, finds evidence that General James Mattoon Scott (Burt Lancaster), the wildly popular head of the Joint Chiefs and certain Presidential candidate in two years, is not planning to wait. Casey goes to the president with the information and a web of intrigue begins with each side unsure of who can be trusted and who can't. Mostly, it is who can't be trusted. Ava Gardner has a small but important role[56] as a woman who may have information that would damage General Scott.

This is a very good political film directed by John Frankenheimer, who also directed *The Manchurian Candidate*, perhaps the greatest film about politics ever made. Lancaster is at his best as the hard-driving general, March is good as the resolute president who is tougher than we think, and Douglas is noteworthy as the colonel who thinks there is something wrong in the State of Denmark. An absolutely terrific supporting cast includes Martin Balsam, Edmond O'Brien, Hugh Marlowe, Andrew Duggan, and Whit Bissell, who is finally playing something besides a store clerk in the Old West.

Burt Lancaster and Kirk Douglas were good friends on and off screen.

---

56 Her scenes were shot in six days

They appeared in seven films together between 1947's *I Walk Alone* and 1986's *Tough Guys*. My all-time favorite collaboration of theirs was probably the 1957 Western *Gunfight at the OK Corral*, with Lancaster as Wyatt Earp and Douglas as Doc Holliday.

Kirk Douglas as Doc Holliday and Burt Lancaster as Wyatt Earp about to confront the Clantons and Johnny Ringo in *Gunfight at the O.K. Corral*. They were both terrific in this film. And guess what? Whit Bissell plays a storekeeper, of course.

6. *The Snows of Kilimanjaro* - 1952

As writer Harry Street (Gregory Peck) lies gravely wounded from an African hunting accident near the base of Mount Kilimanjaro, he feverishly reflects on what he perceives as his failures at love and writing. The movie is based on the novel by Ernest Hemingway and at least somewhat autobiographical. Through his delirium he recalls his one true love Cynthia Green (Ava Gardner), whom he lost by his obsession for roaming the world in search of stories for his novels. Though she is now deceased, Cynthia continues to haunt Street's thoughts. In spite of one successful novel after another, Street feels he has compromised his talent to ensure the success of his books, making him a failure in his eyes. His neglected wife Helen (Susan Hayward) tends to his wounds, listens to his ranting, endures his talk of lost loves, and tries to restore in him the will to fight his illness until help arrives. Her devotion to him makes him finally realize that he is not a failure.

With his realization of a chance for love and happiness with Helen, he regains his will to live.

While the photography and scenery are first rate, the main problem with this film is that it is pretty boring. It is basically a series of flashbacks on how Harry has messed up his life. Ava Gardner is good as his first wife, who plays her part admirably as a young, not-important woman who wants domesticity not excitement, and who wrecks their union to have a child and eventually drinks herself to death.

Ava Gardner was a rare combination of brains and beauty. From the rural South, she was generally good when given half a chance to act, and really good in several films. I guess the closest actress to her today might be Angelina Jolie.

9. William Holden (1918-1981)

William Holden was an outstanding leading man whose career spanned four decades - from the late 1930s through the late 1970s. He was always a good actor and starred in a number of first-rate classic Hollywood films. Because he generally played an outsider, a renegade, or a non-conformist, you would probably never believe that he was a life-long Republican who was best man at the wedding of his good friends Ronald and Nancy Reagan.

Biography

William Holden was born William Franklin Beedle Jr. on April 17, 1918, in O'Fallon, Illinois, a suburb of St. Louis. His father, a chemist, moved his family to Pasadena when William Jr. was very young. Holden went to school in Monrovia and South Pasadena and attended Pasadena Junior College.

He acted in several radio plays in college, and in 1939 a talent scout got him a small part in the movie *Million Dollar Legs*. At that point he changed his name to Holden, reportedly taking the name of a Los Angeles Times editor with the hope the paper's critics would not pan his first movie performance too severely.

He need not have worried. The camera liked his face and his next role in *Golden Boy* (1939), made him a star. In that film, which was based on a play by Clifford Odets, Holden played Joe Bonaparte, a violinist who becomes a boxer.

"He was handsome, but he looked almost too pretty in that movie," said Times movie critic Sheila Benson. "He had the kind of face that improved over the years. What he came to represent was integrity, the same thing you get from someone like Henry Fonda."

Over the years Holden's rich but unpretentious voice became as distinctive as his increasingly craggy face. He always brought a reassuring presence to any scene. There was the sense that this polite, no-nonsense man was capable of heroics if the need arose.

Holden made more than 50 movies, including *The Wild Bunch*, - a comeback for Holden - *Bridge On the RiverKwai,* and *Picnic*. He also starred in *The Blue Knight*, a TV movie based on the Joseph Wambaugh novel about a Los Angeles cop.

Grover Lewis, a former journalist who studied early Hollywood, said, "Holden didn't get the recognition of stars like Gary Cooper, but you look at the movies he made and you realize that several, especially *Sunset Boulevard* and *The Wild Bunch*, were among the best ever made."[57]

Lewis once interviewed Sam Peckinpah, director of *The Wild Bunch*, a movie about a bunch of misfits in the West at the beginning of the 20th Century who have outlived their time. Peckinpah told Lewis of Holden's role in a key scene. "Holden and Ernest Borgnine are sitting

---

57 I might add *Stalag 17* to that list also.

by a campfire, passing the bottle," said Lewis. "Then they begin talking about their plans to give up the outlaw life. Peckinpah said that the whole crew was crying by the time the scene was over. Nobody could have played that role and given it the resonance Holden did."

It was in *The Bridge On the River Kwai* that Holden most vividly portrayed the American male of the World War II generation. And he played a similar hard-bitten character in the role in *Stalag 17* that won him an Oscar. His fellow prisoners dislike him because he is a hustler looking out for himself, but he plays a crucial role in the prison camp escape at the end. Holden actually served during World War II, although he never saw action. He enlisted in the Army and was graduated a first lieutenant from the Army Air Force Officers Candidate School.

Although he always maintained residences in California, Holden also had houses in Switzerland and in Kenya. He was a conservationist and worked for years to maintain big game habitats on the African continent.

He was not heard from much in the 1960s, when he lived in Switzerland and made several undistinguished films. Then he made a comeback in 1969 with *The Wild Bunch* and was praised for his work in *Network* in 1976.

Holden married actress Brenda Marshall in 1941. They had two children of their own, Peter and Scott, and raised a daughter, Virginia, from Marshall's previous marriage. Holden and his wife separated in 1963 and were later divorced.

Holden died of natural causes on November 16, 1981, apparently from injuries suffered after a fall. In 1982, actress Stefanie Powers, with whom he had been in a relationship since 1975, helped set up the William Holden Wildlife Foundation and the William Holden Wildlife Education Center in Kenya.

Awards

William Holden won an Oscar for Best Actor in 1954 for *Stalag 17*. He was nominated for Best Actor for *Sunset Boulevard* in 1951 but lost out to

Jose Ferrer in *Cyrano de Bergerac* and was also nominated for Best Actor for *Network* in 1977 but lost out to his co-star, Peter Finch, for the same film.

Holden received an Emmy award for Best Lead Actor in a Limited Series for his performance in the 1973 cop movie, *The Blue Knight*. He was also nominated for BAFTA awards for *Picnic* and for *Network* but did not win either time. Holden also won two Golden Apple awards for Most Cooperative Actor in 1951 and 1955.

My Favorite William Holden Films

1. *Sunset Boulevard* - 1950
2. *Stalag 17* - 1953
3. *The Bridge on the River Kwai* - 1957
4. *Born Yesterday* - 1950
5. *The Horse Soldiers* - 1959
6. *The Man from Colorado* - 1948
7. *Golden Boy* - 1939

1. *Sunset Boulevard* - 1950

In Hollywood around 1950, the obscure screenplay writer Joe Gillis (William Holden) is not able to sell his work to the studios, is full of debts, and is thinking of returning to his hometown to work in an office. While trying to escape from his creditors and down to only his car, Joe has a flat tire and parks his car in a old run-down mansion on Sunset Boulevard. He meets the owner and former silent-movie star Norma Desmond (Gloria Swanson, in the performance of a lifetime), who lives alone with her butler and driver Max Von Mayerling (former director Erich von Stroheim). Norma is demented and believes she will return to the cinema industry, and is protected and isolated from the world by Max, who was her director and husband in the past and still loves her; Norma especially wants to get back with her favorite director, Cecil B. DeMille. Norma proposes Joe move to the mansion and help her in writing a screenplay for her comeback to the cinema, and the small-time writer becomes her lover and gigolo. But when Joe falls in love with young aspiring writer Betty Schaefer (Nancy Olson), Norma becomes jealous and goes completely insane, and her madness leads to a tragic end for several people.

Sunset Boulevard really struck a chord with audiences and critics alike and continues to be a huge hit with classic movie fans.[58] Lots of famous lines in this film, including Joe saying something like "You're Norma Desmond. You used to be big in pictures" and her responding "I am big. It's the pictures that got small." There are many reasons to watch this film, most notably to watch Norma Desmond's decline from being simply out of touch to complete insanity. Her descent down the staircase in the movie's film scene is one of the most treasured scenes in film annals, and she is scary in that scene.

Sunset Boulevard grossed over $5.3 million, quite a good sum for that era. It won three Oscars, for Best Writing, Best Art Direction, and Best Musical Score; it was nominated for eight others, including Best Picture, Best Actor (Holden) Best Actress (Swanson), and Best Director (the great Billy Wilder). For Best Picture, it lost out to *All About Eve*, certainly an outstanding film in its own right. I can't really understand how Gloria Swanson lost out to Judy Holliday in *Born Yesterday*, but she did. And Holden was really good as the down-on-his-luck screen writer who bites off more than he can chew and ends up in the swimming pool.

Paramount was a bit afraid of the Hollywood critics, so the film actually opened in Evanston, Illinois in late 1949 before making its official opening at Radio City Music Hall a bit later.

Billy Wilder was one of the greatest directors in the history of Hollywood. In addition to *Sunset Boulevard*, his films included *The Apartment, Some Like it Hot, Witness for the Prosecution, Stalag 17, The Lost Weekend,* and *Double Indemnity* - some of the greatest films in Hollywood history. He won six Academy Awards in his illustrious career, which

---

58 Deemed "culturally, historically, or aesthetically significant" by the U.S. Library of Congress in 1989, *Sunset Boulevard* was included in the first group of films selected for preservation in the National Film Registry. In 1998, it was ranked number 12 on the American Film Institute's list of the 100 best American films.

included surviving working with a difficult Marilyn Monroe. Not bad for a guy who emigrated to America in 1933 to escape Hitler, and who did not know a word of English when he came here.

Charles Brackett (Producer of *Sunset Boulevard*), Gloria Swanson, and Director Billy Wilder, on right, in publicity photos for the film.

2. *Stalag 17* - 1953

Another classic William Holden film that depicts life in a German prisoner of war camp during World War II, as American POW's are held by their German captors.[59]

It is Christmas 1944 for the American POWs in Stalag 17. And to compound the problem of depression, the men in Barracks four, all sergeants, have to deal with a grave problem - there seems to be a security leak (a stoolie) in their barracks. How do they know that? The Germans always seem to be forewarned about escapes and in the most recent attempt the two men, Manfredi and Johnson, walked straight into a trap and were killed. For some in Barracks four, especially the loud-mouthed Duke (Neville Brand), the leaker is obvious: J.J. Sefton

---

59 "Stalag" means prisoner of war camp in German.

(William Holden), a wheeler-dealer loner who does not hesitate to trade with the guards and who has acquired goods and privileges that no other prisoner seems to have.

Sefton denies giving the Germans any information and makes it quite clear that he has no intention of ever trying to escape. He plans to ride out the war in what little comfort he can arrange, but it does not include spying for the Germans. As tensions mount and a mob mentality against Sefton takes root, it becomes obvious that Sefton will have to find the real snitch if he is to have any peace and avoid the beatings Duke and the others give him. At the same time, a newly-incarcerated lieutenant (Don Taylor) plans another escape. Eventually, Sefton finds the secret, which leads to uncovering the real traitor.

Stalag 17 is a really good WWII film that takes place away from the battlefield and instead inside a POW camp. [60] Holden is the key to the story - he is extremely cynical yet very brave. Finding humor in the midst of a POW camp with a traitor in the midst is a difficult thing to pull off, but Director Billy Wilder manages to handle it admirably. A superb supporting cast includes Neville Brand, Robert Strauss, Peter Graves, Harvey Lembeck, and Richard Erdman, one of whom is the traitor; but it's Holden's nearly impossible mission to find the real traitor.

William Holden won a well-deserved 1954 Best Actor Oscar for *Stalag 17*, beating out Burt Lancaster for *From Here to Eternity* and Marlon Brando in *Julius Caesar*, among others. Robert Strauss as the loudmouth Sgt. "Animal" Kuzawa was nominated for Best Supporting Actor (losing out to Frank Sinatra in *From Here to Eternity*), and Billy Wilder was also nominated for Best Director but lost out to Eternity's Fred Zinnimann.[61]

Neville Brand was a very interesting individual. Though he was almost

---

60 The 1960s television comedy *Hogan's Heroes* is loosely based on this film.

61 Overall *From Here to Eternity* was clearly the superior film, although both dealt with World War II.

always the gruff bad guy in movies, in real life he was the fourth most decorated soldier in WWII and also had one of the largest private libraries in the United States with over 30,000 books at one time.

Neville Brand, on the right, menacing Whit Bissell. Hard to believe this guy was an avid reader who owned over 30,000 books, but it's true!

3. *The Bridge on the River Kwai* - 1957

The Bridge on the River Kwai opens in a Japanese prisoner-of-war camp in Burma in 1943 in the middle of World War II, where a battle of wills rages between camp commander Colonel Saito (Sessue Hayakawa) and newly arrived British colonel Nicholson (Alec Guinness). Saito insists that Nicholson order his men to build a bridge over the river Kwai, which will be used to transport Japanese munitions. Nicholson refuses, despite all the various "persuasive" devices at Saito's disposal. Finally, Nicholson agrees, not so much to cooperate with his captor as to provide a morale-boosting project for the military engineers under his command. The colonel will prove that, by building a better bridge than Saito's men could build, the British soldier is a superior being even when under the thumb of the enemy.

As the bridge goes up, Nicholson becomes obsessed with completing it to perfection, eventually losing sight of the fact that it will really only benefit the Japanese. Meanwhile, American POW Shears (William Holden), having escaped from the camp, agrees to save himself from a

101

court martial by leading a group of British soldiers back to the camp to destroy Nicholson's bridge. Upon his return, Shears realizes that Nicholson's mania to complete his project has driven him mad.

William Holden gives a strong performance but this is really Alec Guinness' film. The cinematography, screenplay, and editing were all superb, as was the music. And who can forget the song, "The Colonel Bogey March," which was actually written as a march for British soldiers in 1914, not for this film, but was at least partially used in *Bridge*.

Filmed in Ceylon, *The Bridge on the River Kwai* won seven Academy Awards, including Best Picture, Best Director for the legendary British filmmaker David Lean (who also directed *Lawrence of Arabia*), and Best Actor for Guinness. It also won Best Screenplay for Pierre Boulle, the author of the novel on which the film was based, even though the actual writers were blacklisted writers[62] Carl Foreman and Michael Wilson, who were given their Oscars under the table.

4. *Born Yesterday* - 1950

1950 was obviously a very good year for William Holden, as both *Sunset Boulevard* and *Born Yesterday* were made that year.

Uncouth, loud-mouth junkyard tycoon Harry Brock (Broderick Crawford) descends upon Washington D.C. to buy himself a congressman or two, bringing with him his mistress, ex-showgirl Billie Dawn (Judy Holliday, in her Oscar-winning performance). Brock hires

---

62 The Hollywood blacklist - as the broader entertainment industry blacklist is generally known - was the practice of denying employment to screenwriters, actors, directors, musicians, and other American entertainment professionals during the mid-20th century because they were accused of having Communist ties or sympathies. The blacklist began in 1947 and ended in 1960, when *Spartacus* producer and star Kirk Douglas insisted that screenwriter Dalton Trumbo's name be listed as the screenwriter in the film's credits.

newspaperman Paul Verrall (William Holden) to see if he can soften her rough edges and make her more presentable in Washington society.

But Harry gets more than he bargained for as Billie absorbs Verall's lessons in U.S. history, and Billie not only comes to the realization that Harry is nothing but a two-bit, corrupt crook, but in the process also falls in love with her handsome tutor.

Written by the team of Ruth Gordon and Garson Kanin, this romantic comedy is as good as it gets, especially the performance of Judy Holliday as the dumb blond.[63] The film won an Oscar for Holliday as Best Actress and was nominated for four others, including Best Picture and Best Director, but lost out to *All About Eve* in both of those categories. Can't argue with that!

5. *The Horse Soldiers* - 1959

Directed by John Ford and starring John Wayne and William Holden, this Civil War tale begins when a Union Cavalry outfit is sent behind Confederate lines under the command of Colonel John Marlowe (John Wayne) to cut supply lines by destroying a rail/supply center. Along with them is sent an insolent doctor (William Holden) who causes instant antipathy between him and the commander. The secret plan for the mission is overheard by a southern belle (Constance Towers) who with her maid, (former tennis champion Althea Gibson) must be taken along to assure their silence. The Union officers each have different reasons for wanting to be on the mission.

Not a big hit with either the critics or public, the film nevertheless includes strong performances by both John Wayne and William Holden. During filming, veteran stuntman Fred Kennedy died after falling from a horse and breaking his neck; John Ford was so devastated he lost interest in the film after that, perhaps a factor in its lack of success.

6. *The Man from Colorado* - 1948

---

63   In reality, Judy Holliday supposedly had an IQ of 172, making her anything but a dumb blonde in real life.

Not one of William Holden's greatest films, to be sure, but a good western that co-stars best friends in real life, William Holden and Glenn Ford, two of the biggest stars of the 1950s. They often competed for the same parts but nevertheless remained close friends - as well as staunch Republicans - until Holden's death in 1981.

Two friends return home after their discharge from the army after the Civil War. However, one of them, Owen Devereaux (Glenn Ford) has had deep-rooted psychological damage due to his experiences during the war, and as his behavior becomes more erratic - and violent - his friend Del Stewart (William Holden) desperately tries to find a way to help him.

Devereaux and his friend Stewart have been through the whole war together, but Stewart has managed to retain a sense of balance despite the horrors he has seen. Devereaux, on the other hand, is on a slippery slope. Even after an atrocity at the very beginning of the film - Union Officer Devereaux ordering his men to fire on Confederate soldiers despite the fact that the Confederates have held up the white flag to surrender - he is still aware of his act of cruelty and writes in his diary about it. He can't control himself anymore.

Unfortunately, Devereux goes on to a career as a Federal prosecutor because of his tough stance on law enforcement. That works for a while, but he eventually becomes unglued and starts ordering inhumane attacks against miners and other local folks to the dismay of his friend Stewart and others.

This is really more of a Glenn Ford than a William Holden film, but it pairs the two in one of their two films together. As I said, they were often rivals for the same parts but remained close friends for their entire adult lives. Ellen Drew as their mutual love interest, Ray Collins (Lieutenant Tragg from the *Perry Mason* television series), Edgar Buchanan, and Jerome Courtland complete the cast.

> The story goes - apparently true - that Ford and Holden used to both stuff newspaper in their shoes to make themselves look taller. But they mutually decided to stop this practice after it got too uncomfortable.

I can only think of two westerns in which Glenn Ford was the villain - this film and the aforementioned *3:10 To Yuma*. In the 1953 Western, *The Man from the Alamo*, everyone thought he was the heel, because he left the Alamo early; but in fact, he was sent by his fellow Texans to see how their families were doing.

William Holden and Glenn Ford in a publicity photo from *The Man from Colorado*. **By the way, both men were 5'11".**

7. *Golden Boy* - 1939

Golden Boy was William Holden's third film and first starring role at age 21 as violinist turned boxer Joe Bonaparte. Joe Bonaparte's father (the great Lee J. Cobb) wants him to pursue his musical talent; but Joe wants to be a boxer. Persuading near-bankrupt manager Tom Moody (Adolphe Menjou) to give him a chance, Joe quickly rises in his new profession. When he has second thoughts Moody's girl Lorna (the even greater Barbara Stanwyck) uses her charm to keep him boxing. But when tough gangster Eddie Fuseli (Joseph Calleia) wants to "buy a piece" of Joe, Lorna herself begins to have second thoughts; down deep, she has a heart of gold and really cares for Joe. Is it too late?

Golden Boy is the film that made William Holden a star. However, the producers at Columbia Pictures were initially unhappy with Holden's work and tried to dismiss him from the film, but Barbara Stanwyck insisted that he be retained. Thirty-nine years later, when Holden and Stanwyck were joint presenters at the 1978 Academy Awards, he interrupted their reading of a nominee list to publicly thank her for saving his career. Nice gesture!

As you can see, William Holden was a top-notch leading man in a career that lasted over 40 years. Though I would not call him a great actor, he was a pretty darn good one and starred in three of the best films of that era - *Sunset Boulevard, Stalag 17,* and *The Bridge on the River Kwai.* And let's not forget his starring role in a great Western that is not covered by the years included in this book - *The Wild Bunch* (1969), with Holden as Pike Bishop headlining a great cast about a group of old outlaws in the early 20th century going after one last job (and of course, it is their last job).

10. Virginia Mayo (1920-2005)

Virginia Mayo was the picture of All-American blonde prettiness who alternated between comedies and dramas, playing both the good girl and the villain, and starring versus supporting roles with ease. She was Danny Kaye's dream girl in four Samuel Goldwyn technicolor musicals in the 1940s, and, at Warner Brothers in the 1950s, she starred in relatively lightweight films but always remained in the limelight.

However, there was more to Mayo than met the eye. When given the chance to act, she was really very good, as in two of Raoul Walsh's best films, the gangster drama *White Heat*, and the western *Colorado Territory* (both 1949). In that year, six of her films were released, and she continued to be a popular star for another 10 years in a variety of genres. Perhaps *She's Working Her Way Through College* (1952), in which Mayo plays Hot Garters Gertie, a burlesque star with ambitions to be a serious actress, who enrolls in a drama course, was somewhat autobiographical.

Biography

Virginia May was born Virginia Clara Jones in St Louis, Missouri on November 30, 1920. One of her ancestors fought in the American Revolution and later founded the city of East St Louis, Illinois. Her aunt, sister to Virginia's journalist father, ran a dance studio, where Virginia took lessons from the age of six. After graduating from high school in 1937, she became a member of the corps-de-ballet of the St Louis Municipal Opera. She then became a show girl in a Broadway revue, where she was spotted by an MGM talent scout.

David O. Selznick gave her a screen test, but decided not to sign her. But Samuel Goldwyn saw her potential, making her one of his Goldwyn Girls, as well as immediately giving her a small speaking part in *Jack London* (1943), which starred the uncharismatic Michael O'Shea in the title role. O'Shea and Mayo were married four years later, the marriage lasting until his death in 1973.

Mayo soon graduated from the ranks of the Goldwyn Girls to be Bob Hope's co-star in *The Princess And The Pirate* (1944), in which she looked ravishing in color and had good comic timing. At the end, Hope loses Mayo to Bing Crosby, who appears in a cameo for a few seconds. "How do you like that!" responded Hope, "I knock myself out for nine reels and some bit player from Paramount comes over and gets the girl. That's the last film I do for Goldwyn." So it was.

Goldwyn then cast his two favorites, Mayo and Danny Kaye, in *Wonder Man* (1944), in which she was a sweet librarian to his bookworm with a gangster twin brother. In *The Kid From Brooklyn* (1946), cream puff milkman Kaye wins Mayo and the middleweight boxing championship of the world. She appears in Kaye's daydreams in *The Secret Life Of Walter Mitty* (1947), and, later in Mitty's real life, in need of rescuing from evil Boris Karloff. By that time, "leggy Mayo with her voluptuous body and creamy skin"[64] was part of many male filmgoers' fantasies.

---

64 From Virginia Mayo's biography in *The Guardian*.

So it was brilliant casting against type when she took the role of Dana Andrews's unsympathetic, floozy wife in William Wyler's multiple Oscar-winner, *The Best Years Of Our Lives* (1946), about returning war veterans.

Mayo then brought her talent for drama to the role of the sensuous saloon singer on the run with escaped convict Joel McCrea in Raoul Walsh's *Colorado Territory*, an intense tale of doomed love. The ending, as the lovers choose to die together in the barren rockscape, is one of the great western climaxes.

Walsh again got the best out of her in *White Heat*, a classic gangster movie, in which she was the flighty wife of psychopath James Cagney, competing with his mother for his affection. In 1950 she danced gleefully with Cagney in *The West Point Story*. She was also a spirited heroine in period pieces, opposite Burt Lancaster in *The Flame And The Arrow* (1950), Gregory Peck in *Captain Horatio Hornblower* (1951), and Alan Ladd in *The Iron Mistress* (1952).

She could do little to enliven *King Richard And The Crusades* (1954), in which, as Lady Edith, she has the line: "Fight, fight, fight! That's all you think of, Dick Plantagenet!"; nor *The Silver Chalice* (1955), where she dallies with Paul Newman in his film debut; nor as Cleopatra in *The Story Of Mankind* (1957), possibly the most foolish film of the decade.

From the mid-1950s on, Mayo was at her best in westerns, often assertive until she changed her tight-fitting riding breeches for something more feminine. Walsh allowed her, as a rustler's daughter, to be more than a match for Kirk Douglas in *Along The Great Divide* (1951). In *Devil's Canyon* (1953), she was a provocatively dressed woman among 500 men in a prison compound. Mayo's last good horse opera was *Westbound* (1959), starring Randolph Scott and directed by Budd Boetticher.

Mayo had been retired for over a decade when she was tempted to return to the screen in a horror picture, *French Quarter* (1978). She made another one, *Evil Spirits* in 1991. The glamour girl, who had not aged much, thanks to plastic surgery, substantiated the idea that blondes have more fun.

Awards

Not exactly an award, but I thought this was funny. Virginia Mayo was once termed "the most beautiful blonde in the world" and her beauty so impressed the Sultan of Morocco than seeing her was "tangible proof of the existence of God."[65]

My Favorite Virginia Mayo Films

I have tried to include a variety of film genres in this category.

1. *The Best Years of Our Lives* - 1946
2. *White Heat* - 1949
3. *The Flame and the Arrow* - 1950
4. *The Secret Life of Walter Mitty* - 1947
5. *Wonder Man* - 1945
6. *The Silver Chalice* -- 1954

1. *The Best Years of Our Lives* - 1946

The Best Years of Our Lives is probably my all-time favorite American film, and Virginia Mayo has an important supporting part in the movie. It concerns the return of three World War II veterans immediately after the war - Fredric March, Dana Andrews, and Harold Russell; Mayo plays the wife of returning pilot Andrews, and she represents a stark contrast to the typical image of the faithful, long-suffering American wife - she is a party girl who has been completely unfaithful to Andrews while he was at war. Right after he gets back and is flushed with cash, things are great; but as soon as troubles start, and he can't find a job, she takes up with a new boyfriend - Steve Cochran - who seems to have no trouble finding and spending money on her. Of course, Dana Andrews eventually breaks up with Mayo and falls in love with his real soulmate - Theresa Wright. The last scene of the film has the two of them kissing, and the viewer guesses that while Andrews has had a tough time readjusting to civilian life, things are slowly starting to go favorably for him.

---

65   International Movie Data Based (IMDB) bio of Virginia Mayo.

The Best Years of Our Lives has a great cast, including Myrna Loy to the people I have already mentioned. It swept all the major Oscars that year. Mayo is terrific as the unfaithful wife;she could easily have been nominated for an Oscar but was not. But it is a really good performance in a serious and unsympathetic role.

Husband Dana Andrews, Wife Virginia Mayo, and boyfriend Steve Cochran in *The Best Years of Our Lives*.You can tell the two guys don't care for each other. About five minutes later, Andrews decides he has had enough, and walks out on his wife.

2. *White Heat* - 1949

Cody Jarrett (James Cagney) is the sadistic leader of a ruthless gang of thieves. Afflicted by terrible headaches and fiercely devoted to his "Ma," (Margaret Wycherly) Cody is a volatile, violent, and eccentric leader. Cody's top henchman (Steve Cochran again) wants to lead the gang and attempts to have an "accident" happen to Cody so he can take over the gang and also Cody's wife Verna (Virginia Mayo in another good role as the two-timing wife), while Cody is running the gang from his jail cell. But Cody is saved by an undercover cop (Edmond O'Brien), who thereby befriends him and infiltrates the gang. Of course, Cody breaks out of jail.

Finally, the stage is set for Cody's ultimate betrayal and downfall, during a big heist at a chemical plant, where in the last scene, Cody yells out, "Made it, Ma. Top of the world.!"

White Heat was clearly James Cagney's film, but Virginia Mayo was also good as a sleazier version of the role she played three years earlier in *The Best Years of Our Lives.White Heat* is a really good crime drama, with Cagney exceptional as the psychotic killer who loves no one except his mother, of course.

3. *The Flame and the Arrow* - 1950

I have always enjoyed Burt Lancaster in swashbucklers, and this film was no exception. He made three of them that I can think of, *His Majesty O'Keefe* and *The Crimson Pirate* (the best of the three) being the other two. Perhaps it was his background as a circus trapeze performer and his superior athletic ability that made him so good in these types of films. Virginia Mayo said this about Lancaster: "He was very intense, but much more likable then Kirk Douglas. He's very intelligent and reads a lot. He used to keep in great shape. He was an acrobat and did his own trapeze work in one of his films."[66]

The Flame and the Arrow is sort of an Italian version of Robin Hood.Twelfth-century Lombardy lies under the iron heel of German overlord Count Ulrich "The Hawk," but in the mountains, guerillas yet resist. Five years before our story, Ulrich stole away the pretty wife of young archer Dardo (Burt Lancaster) who, cynical rather than embittered, still has little interest in joining the rebels. But this changes when his son, too, is taken from him. The rest of the film is lighthearted swashbuckling, plus romantic interludes with lovely hostage Anne (Virginia Mayo).

There are definite similarities to the Robin Hood tale. Just like Maid Marian, Anne starts out hating Dardo and winds up loving him, and Norman Lloyd plays a troubadour who is very similar to Allen-a-Dale in the Robin Hood saga. And Lancaster and Robin Hood's Errol Flynn were equally handsome and dashing. The villain (Count Ulrich) is similar to Basil Rathbone in *Robin Hood* and played by Robert Douglas.

---

66   Virginia Mayo's biography on IMDB

Norman Lloyd is best known for playing the hospital director on television's *St. Elsewhere*. However, I remember him best as the terrorist/Nazi spy in Alfred Hitchcock's 1942 thriller *Saboteur*. As of the writing of this book, Lloyd is 103 and still alive today.

4. and 5. *The Secret Life of Walter Mitty* (1947) and *Wonder Man* (1945)

Virginia Mayo and Danny Kaye appeared in a total of five films together, and these were perhaps the best two; the others were *A Song is Born*, *The Kid from Brooklyn*, and *Up in Arms*. They always worked well together, and Mayo considered Danny Kaye to be a comic genius who taught her a lot about comic timing. Some people, like me, always liked Danny Kaye a lot, while others found that a little Danny Kaye went a long way.

In *The Secret Life of Walter Mitty*, the clumsy Walter Mitty is the publisher of pulp fiction at the New York City-based Pierce Publishing house owned by Bruce Pierce (Thurston Hall). He lives with his overbearing mother (Fay Bainter), and neither his fiancée Gertrude Griswold (Ann Rutherford) and her mother, nor his best friend Tubby Wadsworth (Gordon Jones) respect him. Walter is an escapist and constantly daydreams into a world of fantasy many times during the day (where he plays characters like Error Flynn and Burt Lancaster). When Walter is commuting, he stumbles in the train right into the beautiful Rosalind van Hoorn (Virginia Mayo), who uses Walter to escape from her pursuer. Walter unintentionally gets involved with a dangerous ring of spies that are seeking a black book with notes about a hidden treasure and is constantly getting involved with Mayo (not a bad deal for a guy who is otherwise a nerd).

Loosely based on the 1939 short story by James Thurber, the key difference is that in the short story, the adventures are all daydreams by the Mitty character, while in the film, they become real. But Danny Kaye and Virginia Mayo were a good team, as evidenced by their five films together.

Some people consider 1945's *Wonder Man* to be Danny Kaye's best film, although I prefer *The Court Jester* from 1955 ("The pellet with the poison's in the vessel with the pestle; the chalice from the palace has the brew that is true!)" Energetic, hyper nightclub entertainer Buzzy Bellew (Danny Kaye) was the witness to a murder committed by gangster Ten Grand Jackson - again, we get Steve Cochran! One night, two of Jackson's thugs kill Buzzy and dump his body in the lake at Prospect Park in Brooklyn. Buzzy comes back as a ghost and summons his bookworm twin, Edwin Dingle (also Kaye), to Prospect Park so that he can help the police nail Jackson. Mayo plays Dingle's girlfriend Ellen, who is the local librarian. Again, Kaye and Mayo make a good team, and Kaye in the role of the two very different brothers is absolutely hysterical in this film.

The name of actor Steve Cochran keeps appearing in this chapter on Virginia Mayo. They didn't come much rougher and tougher than he both off and on camera.Throughout post-WWII Hollywood and the 1950s, he played the meanest and sexiest of coldhearted villains, and also had a reputation as a ladies' man off screen. Cochran died suspiciously of a lung infection (acute infectious edema) on his yacht in 1965 at the age of 48, although some people believed that foul play was involved.

6. *The Silver Chalice* - 1954

Paul Newman's first starring role as the Greek artisan Basil is a really stupid film but includes a first-rate performance by Virginia Mayo as the alluring Helena, and an even better one by Jack Palance.

A Greek artisan who is a slave (Paul Newman) is commissioned to cast the chalice of Christ used in The Last Supper in silver, and sculpt the faces of the disciples and of Jesus around its rim. He travels to Jerusalem and eventually to Rome to complete the task. Meanwhile, a nefarious interloper (Jack Palance) is trying to convince the crowds that he is not a mere magician but actually the new Messiah, by using nothing more than cheap magic tricks. Virginia Mayo is sultry and beautiful as Helena, an exotic vixen who tries too hard to be a success. A great supporting cast includes Lorne Green, Pier Angeli, Alexander Scourby, Joseph Wiseman, E.G. Marshall, Michael Pate, and a young Natalie Wood as the young Helena.

Paul Newman considered *The Silver Chalice* to be the worst film he ever made, and his acting was not particularly good at all. But Palance[67] was terrific as the magician who decided he is really a god and attempts to prove it by trying to fly.

If you take a good look at Virginia Mayo's career, she was certainly not typecast in any one particular film genre. She did comedies, dramas, musicals, westerns, and crime films, and was equally good playing heroines or villains. And she was certainly beautiful, as the Sultan of Morocco put it so well.

---

67 Virginia Mayo thought Jack Palance was weird - she was probably correct about that - and did not like working with him at all on this film. Still, she gave a good performance.

11. Dorothy Malone(1924-2018)

I have to admit that I always had a crush on Dorothy Malone, and it's not hard to see why. In fact when I was younger, I thought that next to Marilyn Monroe, and maybe even including Monroe, Dorothy Malone was the most beautiful movie star on the planet. She never quite made it to the status of elite, but she always acquitted herself well on the screen, whether in a starring role or a supporting part. She often played good women who had a past rather than goody two shoes types. Malone was a film star who made an easy transition to television - *Peyton Place* for example. She also had a wonderfully deep sultry voice and a voluptuous figure. Dorothy went from being a brunette to a blonde and amazingly got better movie roles.

Biography

Dorothy Eloise Maloney was born in Chicago, Illinois but was raised in Dallas, Texas. She was one of five children of an accountant who worked for AT&T and moved to Dallas when Dorothy was just six months old. Attending Ursuline Convent and Highland Park High

School, she was quite popular (as "School Favorite"). She was also a noted female athlete while there and won several awards for swimming and horseback riding. Following graduation, she studied at Southern Methodist University with the intent of becoming a nurse, but a role in the college play "Starbound" happened to catch the eye of RKO talent scout Eddie Rubin, and Dorothy was offered a Hollywood contract.

The lovely brunette started off in typical RKO starlet mode with acting/singing/dancing/diction lessons and bit parts (billed as Dorothy Maloney) in such films as the Frank Sinatra musicals *Higher and Higher* (1943) and *Step Lively* (1944), a couple of mysteries in the "Falcon" entries and a showier role in *Show Business* (1944) with Eddie Cantor and George Murphy. RKO lost interest, however, after the two-year contract was up. Warner Brothers then stepped in quickly and offered her a contract.Now billed as Dorothy Malone, her third film offering with the studio finally injected some adrenaline into her floundering young career, when she earned the small role of a seductive book clerk in the Bogart/Bacall classic *The Big Sleep* (1946). Critics and audiences took notice of her small but important part. As a reward, the studio nudged her up the billing ladder with more visible roles in several Westerns, which showed off her equestrian abilities if not her acting skills.

Despite this positive movement, Warner Bros. did not extend Dorothy's contract in 1949 and she returned willingly back to her tightly-knit family in Dallas. Taking a steadier job with an insurance agency, she happened to attend a work-related convention in New York City and grew fascinated with the big city. Deciding to recommit to her acting career, she moved to the Big Apple and studied at the American Theater Wing. In between her studies, she managed to find work on TV, which spurred freelancing movie offers in several films, including the Dean Martin and Jerry Lewis comedy *Scared Stiff* (1953).

Things picked up noticeably once Dorothy went platinum blonde, which seemed to emphasize her sensual beauty. First off was as a sister to Doris Day in *Young at Heart* (1954), a musical remake of *Four Daughters* (1938), back at Warner Bros. She garnered even better attention when she appeared in the war picture *Battle Cry* (1955), in which she shared torrid love scenes (for those times) with film's newest heartthrob Tab Hunter, and continued the momentum with the reliable westerns *Five Guns West* (1955) and *Tall Man Riding* (1955) as well as the non-western *Sincerely Yours* (1955) with Liberace.

By this time Dorothy had signed with Universal. Following a few more westerns for good measure, Dorothy won the role of wild,nymphomaniac Marylee Hadley in the Douglas Sirk soap opera *Written on the Wind* (1956) co-starring Rock Hudson, Lauren Bacall and Robert Stack. Stack and Malone had the showier roles and completely out-shined the two leads, both earning supporting Oscar nominations in the process. Stack lost in his category but Dorothy nabbed the trophy for her splendidly tramp, boozed-up Southern belle which was highlighted by her writhing mambo dance.

Unfortunately, Dorothy's long spell of mediocre filming did not end with all the hoopla she received for *Written on the Wind* (1956). *The Tarnished Angels* (1957), which reunited Malone with Hudson and Stack, faltered, and *Quantez* (1957) with Fred MacMurray was just another run-of-the-mill western. Two major films came her way in *Man of a Thousand Faces* (1957) as the unsympathetic first wife of James Cagney's Lon Chaney Sr, and as alcoholic actress Diana Barrymore in the biographic melodrama *Too Much, Too Soon* (1958), the daughter of John Barrymore, played by Errol Flynn.

At age 35, Dorothy married playboy actor Jacques Bergerac, Ginger Rogers' ex-husband, in 1959. A baby daughter, Mimi, was born the following year. Fewer film offers, which included *Warlock* (1959) and *The Last Voyage* (1960), came her way as Dorothy focused more on family life. While a second daughter, Diane, was born in 1962, Dorothy and Jacques' turbulent marriage did not last and the divorce became final in December of 1964. A bitter custody battle ensued with Dorothy eventually winning primary custody of both daughters.

Television rejuvenated Dorothy's career in the mid-1960s when she earned top billing on TV's first prime time soap opera *Peyton Place* (1964). Dorothy, starring in Lana Turner's 1957 film role of Constance MacKenzie, found herself in a smash hit. The run wasn't entirely happy, however.Doctors discovered blood clots on her lungs which required major surgery and she almost died. Lola Albright filled in until she was able to return. However, the significance of her role dwindled with time and 20th Century-Fox finally wrote her and co-star Tim O'Connor off the show in 1968. Dorothy filed a breach of contract lawsuit which ended in an out-of-court settlement.

Her life on- and off-camera did not improve. Dorothy's second marriage to stockbroker Robert Tomarkin in 1969 lasted only three months, and a third to businessmanCharles Huston Bell managed about three years. Now-matronly roles in the films *Winter Kills* (1979), *Vortex* (1982), *The Being* (1983) and *Rest in Pieces* (1987), were few and far between along with a few TV-movies.

After that, Dorothy Malone settled for good back in Dallas, returning to Hollywood only on occasion. Her last film was a cameo in the popular thriller *Basic Instinct* (1992) as a friend to Sharon Stone. She will be remembered as one of those Hollywood stars who proved she had the talent but somehow got the short end of the stick when it came to quality films offered. She passed away in January 2018 at the age of 93.

Awards
Dorothy Malone won a Best Supporting Actress Oscar in 1957 for *Written on the Wind*. She was nominated for three Golden Globe awards:
- Best Supporting Actress - *Written on the Wind* - 1957
- Best Female TV Star - *Peyton Place* - 1964
- Best Female TV Star - *Peyton Place* - 1965

My Favorite Dorothy Malone Films
1. *Written on the Wind* - 1956
2. *Warlock* - 1959
3. *The Last Sunset* - 1961
4. *Man of a Thousand Faces* - 1957
5. *The Big Sleep* - 1946
6. *Too Much, Too Soon* - 1958
7. *Torpedo Alley* - 1952 - there's a reason for this

1. *Written on the Wind* - 1956

Written on the Wind is an excellent melodrama about a Texas oil family who drive themselves to ruin through lust and greed. Self-destructive, alcoholic nymphomaniac Marylee Hadley (Dorothy Malone) and her insecure, alcoholic playboy brother Kyle (Robert Stack) are the children of Texas oil baron Jasper Hadley (Robert Keith). Spoiled by their inherited wealth and crippled by their personal demons, neither is able to sustain a personal relationship or stay sober, for that matter. Kyle falls in love with and marries Lucy Moore (Lauren Bacall), a beautiful gold-digger. Kyle's geologist friend Mitch Wayne (Rock Hudson) begins a relationship with Marylee. The two relationships wreak havoc on the oil dynasty, resulting in a highly entertaining soap-opera that includes a murder, a trial, and a Perry-Mason type confession.

While the story itself is basically daytime soap opera, Director Douglas Sirk does a commendable job of telling the story, and the acting is first rate all the way. Rock Hudson and Lauren Bacall are the two leads, but Dorothy Malone and Robert Stack are the two who really shine in their roles. Stack was nominated for a best supporting actor Oscar, and Malone won for her performance.

While Robert Stack had almost 100 movie and television roles, today we remember him primarily for playing Eliot Ness on TV's *The Untouchables* from 1959 to 1963.

2. *Warlock* - 1959

This extremely under-rated adult western stars Richard Widmark, Henry Fonda, Anthony Quinn, and Dorothy Malone. In the small frontier mining town of Warlock, rancher Abe McQuown (Tom Drake, who was Judy Garland's boyfriend next door in *Meet Me in St. Louis*) and his gang of cowboy roustabouts, terrorize the peaceful community, humiliating the town's legitimate deputy Sheriff and running him out of town. Helpless and in need of protection, the townsfolk hire the renowned marshal Clay Blaisedell (Henry Fonda), as unofficial Marshal, to bring law and order to the town. Clay arrives with his good friend and backup Tom Morgan (Anthony Quinn).

At his introduction, Blaisedell explains to the town leaders that at first they will be very pleased with him because he will rid the town of McQuown and his rowdies; but after that, when the bad guys are gone, they will come to hate him because he becomes too authoritative for his own good. This happens in every place he goes, apparently. At the same time, Lily Dollar (Dorothy Malone), who has ties to both Blaisedell and Morgan, arrives in town. She hates both men and would do just about anything to see them fail. Of course, the two men stand up to the gang and quiet the town.

Johnny Gannon (Richard Widmark), a former member of the ranch gang, is bothered by the gang's actions, so he reforms and takes on the deputy Sherriff job - the legitimate town lawman - while his brother remains part of the gang. The addition of the official lawman to the mix further complicate matters, as does the budding romance between Widmark and Malone, leading to an inevitable clash of the cowboys, the townsfolk, the gunslingers, and the law.

Warlock is one of my favorite Westerns, and that's saying a lot. Fonda is a good guy who is not really that good of a guy, while Widmark is a bad guy who is really a pretty good guy. And the Quinn character worships Fonda's Blaisedell in a somewhat creepy way. Then, we have Dorothy Malone, with a past with two of the leads and a present with the third. Got that? A superior supporting cast includes Delores Michaels, Richard Arlen, DeForest Kelley (Dr. McCoy on *Star Trek*). Vaughn Taylor, Don Beddoe, and Whit Bissell as a shopkeeper (naturally) in this outstanding adult Western film. And Dorothy Malone shows she is no pushover and more than holds her own against Fonda, Widmark, and Quinn.

3. *The Last Sunset* - 1961

Another good Dorothy Malone western with another cast of stars. Brendan O'Malley (Kirk Douglas) arrives at the Mexican home of old flame Belle Breckenridge (Dorothy Malone) to find her married to a drunkard (Joseph Cotten) getting ready for a cattle drive to Texas. In pursuit of O'Malley is lawman Dana Stribling (Rock Hudson) who has a personal reason for getting him back into his jurisdiction; he wants to bring him back to Texas for the murder of his brother-in-law. Both men decide to join Breckenridge and his wife on the drive.

As they near Texas, one of the principals gets killed and tensions mount, not least because Stribling is starting to court Belle and O'Malley is increasingly drawn by her daughter Missy (Carol Lynley). And the reason for the attraction that O'Malley has for Missy finally comes out. As you might guess, there is the inevitable showdown between Douglas and Hudson as the climax of the film.

Again, Dorothy Malone's character has to battle two strong individuals - Rock Hudson and Kirk Douglas, and a weak husband - Joseph Cotten. She holds her own admirably in a good western. Neville Brand and Jack Elam play their usual slimy bad guys in this film.

4. *Man of a Thousand Faces* - 1957

This bio of legendary silent film star Lon Chaney features James Cagney in a terrific performance as the greatest star of silent films, and Dorothy Malone as his first wife Cleva. The movie takes us through his early years as the son of two deaf parents all the way to his death at the age of 57 of throat cancer.

Cagney gives an unforgettable performance as Lon Chaney in this fascinating true story that follows the life of one of the most iconic and mysterious stars in Hollywood history. Known as the "Man of a Thousand Faces," silent film star Lon Chaney captured the imagination of the world through his incredibly expressive and transformative roles, such as Quasimodo in *The Hunchback of Notre Dame* and the Phantom from the original *Phantom of the Opera*. Behind the scenes, however, this long-suffering talented genius' life was filled with trials and tribulations that helped shape some of his most groundbreaking roles. Among those trials were:

1. His parents were deaf, which required Chaney to develop other methods of communicating with them through gestures.

2. His first wife Cleva, herself a singer and stage performer - and played perfectly by Dorothy Malone - could never deal with his parents and was unstable mentally; she attempted to kill herself by swallowing mercuric chloride while onstage. While the suicide attempt failed, it ended her singing career.

3. The incident forced Chaney to give up his stage career and turn to films, where he was an extra for several years before achieving stardom.

While the entire film is good, the tension between Cagney and Malone as the ill-fated husband and wife, really stands out. We feel for Cleva but find it difficult to understand the choices she made in her life. A really good supporting cast includes Jane Greer, Jim Backus, Robert Evans, Jeanne Cagney as his sister, and Roger Smith as young Creighton Chaney, who became Lon Chaney, Jr.

Dorothy Malone as Cleva Chaney and James Cagney as Lon Chaney in *Man of a Thousand Faces*.

5. *The Big Sleep* - 1946

An early and small but key role for Dorothy Malone in this Humphrey Bogart classic, as a brunette on top of it! Malone plays the Acme Bookstore clerk in the bookstore where private detective Phillip Marlowe (Humphrey Bogart) takes refuge during a thunderstorm. She provided Marlow with information then closes the bookstore and turns down the shades so that she and Bogie can have a tryst.

Based on Raymond Chandler's novel, *The Big Sleep* is the story of private investigator Philip Marlowe, hired by a wealthy general to stop his youngest daughter, Carmen, from being blackmailed about her gambling debts; things almost immediately unravel and blow up from here, as Marlowe finds himself deep within a web of love triangles, blackmail, murder, gambling, and organized crime. Marlowe, with the help of the General's eldest daughter, Vivian (Lauren Bacall), skillfully plots to free the family from this web and trap the main man behind much of this mischief, Eddie Mars (John Ridgely), who meets his end at the hands of his own henchmen.

A classic film noir with Bogart at his best and a very strange plot that has the viewer going "Huh?" on several occasions, Director Howard Hawks reportedly wanted Dorothy for this part because she was so good looking. And she is!

Dorothy Malone and Humphrey Bogart in the Acme Bookstore.

A good supporting cast includes Martha Vickers as Bacall's alcoholic sister, Carmen, as well as veteran character actors Bob Steele and Elisha Cook, Jr.

Veteran character actor Elisha Cook, Jr. appeared in well over 200 movies and television roles. This included roles in such great films as *The Maltese Falcon*, *The Big Sleep*, and *Shane*, where he was the homesteader who challenged Jack Palance and got gunned down. He also appeared as Ice Pick Hofstetler in 13 episodes of *Magnum, P.I.*

> Bob Steele was the king of B westerns in the 30s and 40s, and made supporting appearances in many good movies later in his career, including *Of Mice and Men*, *McClintock*, and *Hang 'em High*.

Western Star Bob Steele in one of his minor B western roles in the 1930s.

6. *Too Much, Too Soon* - 1958

Too Much, Too Soon tells the true story of Diana Barrymore (Dorothy Malone), a theatrical actress who acted on both stage and screen was once part of the legendary Barrymore family. Her father was legendary silent and early sound film star John Barrymore (Errol Flynn), whose own life could have also been called "Too much, too soon." Behind the cameras and backstage, Diana Barrymore would suffer through alcohol and drug abuse, as well as several unsuccessful marriages. Dorothy Malone is excellent in the role of the title character.[68] And Errol Flynn

---

68   The real Diana Barrymore committed suicide at the age of 38.

is surprisingly good as her father, the great John Barrymore. Efrem Zimbalist Jr. (before *77 Sunset Strip* or *The F.B.I*) and Ray Danton head up a strong supporting cast.

7. *Torpedo Alley* - 1952

I said there was a good reason I included this rather mediocre Korean War film, and there is. My dad was in the film! You see, they used a real submarine with a real crew during the making of this film, my dad's submarine during his stint in the Navy during the Korean War, and he got to be in three scenes, along with other crew members.

The film itself is very average. Carrier pilot Lieutenant Bob Bingham (Mark Stevens) is rescued at sea by a submarine after he freezes at the controls and crashes, killing his two crewmen, which he continually blames himself for. He returns to civilian life but soon afterwards, looking for redemption, applies for submarine duty. At the New London, Conn., training base he renews acquaintance with Commander Heywood (James Millican) and Lieutenant Gates (Douglas Kennedy), the skipper and engineering officers of the sub that rescued him at sea. Bingham falls in love with Navy nurse Lieutenant Susan Peabody (Dorothy Malone), daughter of Warrant Officer Peabody (Charles Winninger) and the girl friend of Gates.

Heywood gets a submarine command at the outbreak of the Korean "police action" and Bingham and his friend, Lieutenant Graham (Bill Williams), are part of the officer's group on Heywood's sub. Obviously, Bingham gets a chance to redeem itself, and of course, this is Hollywood, so he does so.

My dad said that Dorothy Malone and Bill Williams in particular were really nice to work with but that Mark Stevens was kind of aloof, standoffish. Williams was the real-life husband of Barbara Hale (Della Street of *Perry Mason*), and Stevens, while a decent actor, never quite made it into the category of A list stars.

So there you have it. Never a star in the way some of the other females were on this list, Dorothy Malone was unbelievably beautiful and sexy, and a darn good actress to boot! She won an Oscar, seemed to be in charge of her own life, and lived to be 93. Not bad!

12. Stewart Granger (1913-1993)

As I have indicated, one of my favorite film genres is the swashbuckler, and Stewart Granger is right up there with Errol Flynn and - to a lesser extent - Louis Hayward - as being the best of the swashbucklers. Appearing in over 75 movies, Granger's successes included *Scaramouche* and a remake of *The Prisoner of Zenda*, as well as countless adventure films, all of which makes him a pretty good forgotten star. And that premature streak of silver/gray hair only seemed to add to his attractiveness.

Biography

Stewart Granger, whose real name was James Lablanche Stewart - I think the name James Stewart was already spoken for - was born May 13, 1913 in London and attended Epsom College. He briefly considered studying medicine, but he changed his mind and entered the Webber-Douglas School of Dramatic Art in London.

After working in repertory theater in Hull and Birmingham, England, he took the role of Captain Hamilton in "The Sun Never Sets" at the Drury Lane Theater in London in 1938. This successful debut was followed by an appearance opposite Vivien Leigh in "Serena Blandish."

After taking a screen test, Stewart Granger made his film debut as the juvenile lead in *So This Is London* in 1938. The next year, he joined the Old Vic Company.

During World War II, Granger served with the Black Watch Regiment from 1940 to 1942, when he was placed on disability as a result of stomach ulcers. After the war, Granger became one of Britain's leading romantic screen stars, appearing in *The Man in Gray* (1943), *Fanny by Gaslight* (1944), *Caesar and Cleopatra* as Apollodorus opposite Vivien Leigh as Cleopatra (1946), and other movies.

He came to the United States in 1950 to star in *King Solomon's Mines*, changing his name to avoid being confused with the film star James Stewart. Executives at MGM were so impressed by his performance that they cast him as the virile leading man in a series of romantic swashbuckling films, including a 1953 remake of *The Prisoner of Zenda* and *Salome* (1953). He played in dozens of romantic films, including *Scaramouche* (1952), *Beau Brummel* (1954) and *Bhowani Junction* (1956).

Stewart Granger became a United States citizen in 1956 but continued to star in films in the United States and Europe. Playing John Wayne's buddy in *North to Alaska*, he also starred with Robert Taylor in two films, *All the Brothers Were Valiant* and *The Last Hunt*, in which Taylor and Granger took turns playing the hero and villain.

In a 1970 interview, Mr. Granger delivered a harsh judgment on his film career. "Stewart Granger was quite a successful film star," he said, "but I don't think he was an actor's actor." Only one film pleased him, he said, *Waterloo Road*, a British film made in 1944, in which he played the heavy. You can actually see in these films that he possessed greater acting ability than the role really called for.

He pointed with pride, however, to his work on the English stage. When asked if he would like to return to the theater, he said: "Too lazy. The theater's hard work."

As his film career began to wane in the 1970's, Granger turned to television. He was among the many actors to portray Sherlock Holmes, starring in a 1972 television movie of *The Hound of the Baskervilles*, and he played the owner of the Shiloh ranch in the last season of *The Virginian* in 1970-1971. In 1991, he played an aging Hollywood actor in an episode of the CBS series *Gabriel's Fire*.

Despite his early experience on the British stage, Stewart Granger did not make his Broadway debut until 1989, in a revival of Somerset Maugham's play "The Circle" with Rex Harrison and Glynis Johns. He stayed with the play when it moved to London, acting opposite Rosemary Harris.

In 1981, he published his autobiography, *Sparks Fly Upward*.

Stewart Granger was married and divorced three times. His first wife was the actress Elspeth March, the second Jean Simmons, the third Viviane Lecerf. He is survived by three daughters and a son. Granger passed away on August 16, 1993 at age 80 of prostate cancer.

Awards

Stewart Granger was nominated for six BAMBI awards and won two. The Bambi Awards have been presented annually since 1948 by Hubert Burda Media to recognize excellence in international media and television, awarded to personalities in the media, arts, culture, sports and other fields "with vision and creativity who affected and inspired the German public that year," both domestic and foreign.

My Favorite Stewart Granger Films

Granger was primarily known for swashbuckler and adventure films, so there are a lot of them in this list. I have also included the two films he made with Robert Taylor and the one he made with John Wayne, because I enjoyed all three movies.

1. *Scaramouche* - 1952
2. *The Prisoner of Zenda* - 1952
3. *King Solomon's Mines* - 1950
4. *North to Alaska* - 1960
5. *The Last Hunt* - 1956
6. *All the Brothers Were Valiant* - 1953
7. *Caesar and Cleopatra* - 1945

1. *Scaramouche* - 1952

Scaramouche is right up there with my all-time favorite swashbuckler films, including *Robin Hood*, *The Man in the Iron Mask* (Louis Hayward version), *The Mark of Zorro*, and *Captain Blood*. Andre-Louis Moreau (Stewart Granger) is a nobleman's bastard son at the time of the French revolution. Noel, the Marquis de Maynes (a very despicable Mel Ferrer), a nobleman in love with the Queen (Nina Foch), is ordered to seek the hand of a young ingenue, Aline (a very beautiful Janet Leigh), in marriage. Andre also meets Aline, and falls in love with her. But when the marquis kills his best friend Phillippe (Richard Anderson, before his days on *Perry Mason* or *The Six Million Dollar Man*) Andre declares himself the Marquis's enemy and vows to avenge his friend.

He hides out, a wanted man, as an actor in a commedia troupe in which his girl friend Lenore (Eleanor Parker) performs, as Scaramouche, a stock clown character, and spends his days learning how to handle a sword. When the troupe moves to Paris, Dr. Dubuque (John Litel), a deputy of the new National Assembly, seeks his help. The aristocrats in the assembly are systematically killing off the deputies representing the common people by provoking them into duels. Moreau is not interested, until Dubuque mentions that de Maynes is one of the duelists. Then he eagerly accepts the seat of a deceased deputy. Each day, he shows up at the assembly to challenge de Maynes, only to find his enemy absent on trivial but official duties, arranged by Aline and Lenore working together to protect the man they both love. However, other nobles in the National Assembly are eager to fight the newcomer, challenging him on a daily basis. Moreau wins each duel, gaining valuable experience with the sword in the process. Eventually Moreau and de Mayne meet in what is probably the longest sword fight in movie history.

Granger is spectacular as a nobody who becomes a first-rate swordsman; he has the perfect blend of hero and con artist to make this film work, and he does an outstanding job in this performance. The rest of the cast is also good, and Granger has to decide between Eleanor Parker and Janet Leigh. What a lucky guy!

Stewart Granger (right) and Mel Ferrer in probably the longest swordfight in the history of sound films, in *Scaramouche*.

2. *The Prisoner of Zenda* - 1952

Not as good as the 1937 version with the incomparable Ronald Colman in the title role, but still good enough in its own right with Stewart Granger in the dual role of King Rudolf V of Ruritania and Rudolf Rassendyll, an English tourist and distant cousin of the king. While they obviously look like twins, the king is a pompous jerk while Rassendyll is a decent human being. By the way, this version is virtually a line-by-line match of the earlier Ronald Colman version.

English trout fisherman Rudolf Rassendyll (Stewart Granger) is about the only tourist not coming to Ruritania for the coronation of Central-European King Rudolf V at Strelsau, but he happens to be a distant relative and is approached because of his uncanny resemblance to the king. His advisors want Rassendyll to just act as a stand in for the oft-drunken king, in order to prevent his envious half-brother Michael (Robert Douglas, who arranged spiking his wine), from seizing the throne when the reputedly less-than-dutiful Rudolf stays away. The ceremony goes well, and he gets acquainted with the charming royal bride, princess Flavia (a beautiful Deborah Kerr), but afterward the king is found to be abducted; so Rassendyll must continue the charade. Once they find the place where the king is being held, the castle of Zenda, Rassendyll is involved in the fight between political parties for control of the prisoner Rudolf V, his throne and his bride, while a formidable third candidate, Michael's disloyal co-conspirator Rupert of Hentzau (the always-good James Mason), is waiting in the curtains for his chance to take over.

The Prisoner of Zenda is an excellent swashbuckler, with swordfights, double crosses, and conspiracies all over the place. Granger is not really the equal of Ronald Colman - who would be? - but is still very good in his own right. And this version is in color, which is a definite upgrade over the 1937 film. The supporting cast includes Louis Calhern and Jane Greer.

Louis Calhern was in a ton of really good movies, including *The Magnificent Yankee* and *Julius Caesar*, where he played the title character. But he is perhaps best known for being the brunt of the Marx Brothers jokes in their best film, *Duck Soup*.

Chico and Harpo - where's Groucho? with Louis Calhern in *Duck Soup* (1933).

3. *King Solomon's Mines* - 1950

Allan Quatermain (Stewart Granger), an experienced hunter and guide, reluctantly agrees to help Elizabeth Curtis (Deborah Kerr) and her brother John Goode (Richard Carlson) search for her husband, who disappeared in the unexplored African interior while searching for the legendary mines of King Solomon. A tall, mysterious native, Umbopa (Siriaque), joins the safari. Allan has no use for women on a safari, but during the long and grueling journey, he and Elizabeth begin to fall in love - no surprise here.

The party encounters Van Brun (Hugo Haas), a lone white man living with a tribe, and learn that he has encountered Curtis. However, when Allan realizes that Van Brun is a fugitive who cannot afford to let them go, they take Van Brun hostage in order to leave the village safely. Van Brun tries to shoot Allan, killing his faithful right-hand man Khiva (Kimursi). But Allan dispatches Van Brun and the party flees from the angry villagers.

When they finally reach the region where the mines are supposed to be, they are met by people who resemble Umbopa. They discover that their companion is royalty; he has returned to attempt to dethrone the evil King Twala (Baziga). The three Anglo Saxons experience a series of additional adventures in this exciting adventure film.

It is interesting to note that the studio wanted Errol Flynn to star in this film, but once he accepted another part, Stewart Granger was selected. The film won Oscars for Best Cinematography, which was beautiful, and Best Editing. It was nominated for Best Picture, but lost out to *All About Eve*, and rightfully so. The film made a profit of over $4 million, making it MGM's most profitable film of 1950.

4. *North To Alaska* - 1960

North To Alaska is an interesting John Wayne/Stewart Granger buddy western, with Stewart Granger playing the second lead to Wayne.. During the Alaskan Gold Rush, partners Sam McCord (John Wayne) and George Pratt (Stewart Granger) strike gold. George sends Sam to Seattle to bring George's fiancée back to Alaska. Sam finds she is already married, and returns instead with Angel (Capucine), a dance hall hostess. Sam, after trying to get George and Angel together, finally romances Angel, who, in the meantime, is busy fighting off the advances of George's younger brother, Billy (Fabian)[69]. Enter Frankie Canon (the great Ernie Kovacs), a local can man who is trying to steal the partners' gold claim.

North To Alaska is as much of a comedy as a Western, but works because of the chemistry between the two leads. People often forget what a good comedic actor John Wayne was, especially when he did not take himself too seriously, and he certainly proves it in this film.

Ernie Kovacs was a true comic genius who was way ahead of his time. His 1961-1962 television show, *The Ernie Kovacs Show*, featured many bizarre sketches, my favorite being The Nairobi Trio, a trio of apes who played music and clobbered each other. Kovacs was married to singer/actress Edie Adams and died in a car accident in 1962 at age 42. What a loss!

Ernie Kovacs and Edie Adams

5. *The Last Hunt* - 1956

---

69 Was it really necessary to cast singer Fabian as Stewart Granger's younger brother? I guess they were trying to appeal to a younger crowd, but Fabian was not really much of an actor. In reality, Granger was thirty years older than Fabian, who really can't act. I know I am repeating myself, but it needs repeating.

In these next two films, Stewart Granger and heartthrob Robert Taylor[70] take turns playing hero and villain. This film is a western while the next one is more of a sea story.

Set in the Badlands of South Dakota in the early 1880s, this is the story of one of the last buffalo hunts in the Northwest. Sandy McKenzie (Stewart Granger) is tired of hunting buffalo, and tired of killing; his old friend Charlie Gilson (Robert Taylor), on the other hand, relishes the hunt and enjoys killing buffalo almost as much as he enjoys killing Indians[71]. To Gilson, one less buffalo is one less Indian, his hatred of the Indian born out when he gets a chance to kill any Indians that get in his way. When Charlie kills an Indian raiding party, and takes a squaw (Debra Paget)[72] as his own, tension develops between the two hunters, and matters will only be settled in a showdown.

Stewart Granger as the hero is pretty good but Robert Taylor as the villain was even better. As Charlie Gilson, Taylor showed that when given half a chance, he was actually not a bad actor at all. Lloyd Nolan and a young Russ Tamblyn head up a fine supporting cast, and the photography is beautiful.

> Debra Paget played a Native American in at least two other westerns that I can think of, *Broken Arrow* and *White Feather*. Her sister, Lisa Gaye. was also an actress.

---

70 Nicknamed "The Man with the Perfect Profile," Robert Taylor was at or near the top male box office star between the late 1930s and mid 1950s. Yet no one under 50 has heard of him today, which is why he was one of the 25 forgotten stars in my first book.

71 The introduction to this film indicated that there were 60 million bison in the West in 1853 and only 30,000 left 30 years later.

72 I'm sure it was the high cheekbones, but Debra Paget certainly played a lot of Native American women!

Stewart Granger, right, and Robert Taylor, background, with Joe De Santis in *The Last Hunt*. Taylor is already scowling. And later, he will have an icy look on his face, if you get my drift.

6. *All the Brothers Were Valiant* - 1953

In this 1953 film, Robert Taylor is the hero (Joel Shore) and Stewart Granger (Mark Shore) is the bad brother. *All the Brothers Were Valiant* is asea-faring saga of two brothers (Taylor and Granger) and the woman they both love (Ann Blyth). Set against South Pacific islands, this love triangle pits one brother against the other as they squabble over Blyth and a bag of pearls on the floor of a lagoon. While Taylor is the captain of the ship, Granger seems to think he can take anything he wants from his brother.

Not really a great script, and not great acting, but it is still interesting to watch two stars like Taylor and Granger in the same film, plus the beautiful Ann Blyth. Keenan Wynn and James Whitmore co-star.

> If you are wondering where you saw Keenan Wynn and James Whitmore together in the same film, it is probably as the two thugs, Lippy and Slug, in the Cole Porter musical *Kiss Me Kate*, where they sing "Brush Up Your Shakespeare."

7. *Caesar and Cleopatra* - 1945

Basically an adaptation of the stage play by George Bernard Shaw, *Caesar and Cleopatra* basically chronicles the arrangement made between Julius Caesar (Claude Rains) and Cleopatra (Vivien Leigh). Cleopatra hasn't been on the throne of Egypt very long when Roman general Caesar pays a visit. Caesar finds the prospect of romance more tempting than he expected, since Cleopatra is a rare woman who is bright as well as beautiful. And for Cleopatra, a friendly relationship with the most powerful man in the world may pay dividends in the future. Stewart Granger is Apollodorus, the third lead, a follower of Cleopatra who is at least somewhat in love with her but pales in comparison to Caesar when it comes to influence and power.

Caesar andCleopatra is basically a filmed version of a stage play. Very talky and not much action. The two leads are good, but the film itself is OK at best. Not a lot takes place, but it is one of the first instances of Stewart Granger having a lead role.

Stewart Granger was a dashing leading man who made a number of really good films, especially during the 1950s. Not a great actor, but definitely serviceable when he got the chance.

13. Deborah Kerr (1921-2007)

Deborah Kerr was an excellent actress, combining brains and beauty in a number of award-winning roles. She was the star of my mother's all-time favorite film - *An Affair to Remember* - what else? as well as several other Oscar-winning as well as big budget films. Born in Glasgow, Scotland, Kerr was mainly a film actress and a good one, but she also did some television work late in her career. She will always be remembered for a handful of roles in some great classic films. And while she generally tended to play a prim and proper female in her movies, apparently she was not at all like that in real life. So in essence, she was ladylike, yet beautiful and sexy at the same time. And she had one of most famous kisses in cinema history - with Burt Lancaster on the beach in *From Here to Eternity*.

Biography

Born Deborah Jane Kerr-Trimmer on September 30, 1921 in Glasgow, Scotland, Deborah Kerr was the daughter of a soldier who had been gassed in World War I. A shy, insecure child, she began as a ballet dancer but found an outlet for expressing her feelings through acting in school. Her aunt, a radio star, got her some stage work when she was a teenager in regional British theaters. There, she came to the attention of British film producer Gabriel Pascal, who cast her in his film version of George Bernard Shaw's *Major Barbara* in 1941.

From there, she made two memorable appearances in films by British directing duo Michael Powell and Emetic Pressburger - in roles as the hero's love interests in *The Life and Death of Colonel Blimp* (1943), then as sister superior to a group of nuns facing temptation in the Himalayas in the fantasy *Black Narcissus* (1947). She also was one of those who entertained British soldiers during World War II.

The latter film brought her to the attention of Hollywood. In 1947 she "crossed the pond" and came to MGM, where she found success in films like *The Hucksters* (1947), *Edward, My Son*(1949) and *Quo Vadis* (1951) She appeared opposite some of the era's biggest stars, including Robert Mitchum, David Niven, Stewart Granger and Spencer Tracy - and worked with many top directors, including John Huston, Otto Preminger and Elia Kazan.

Moving into the 1950s, Deborah Kerr tired of being typecast in serene, ladylike roles, so she rebelled to win a release from her MGM contract and got the plum role of Karen Holmes, the alcoholic, sex-starved army wife who has a fling with Burt Lancaster in the 1953 multi-Oscar Award winning *From Here to Eternity*. And of course, there was *The King and I* with Yul Brynner in 1956.

Then in 1957, she got her biggest break of all when she and Cary Grant played star-crossed lovers who arrange to meet atop the Empire State Building in the enduring - and much-imitated[73] - romance *An Affair to Remember*.

Kerr had a reputation as a "no problem" actress, which directors really liked.[74]"I have never had a fight with any director, good or bad," she

---

73 See *Sleepless in Seattle*, with Tom Hanks and Meg Ryan.

said toward the end of her career. "There is a way around everything if you are smart enough."[75]

After *The Arrangement* in 1968, Kerr took what she called a "leave of absence" from acting, saying she felt she was "either too young or too old" for any role she was offered. But instead she switched to the stage, acting in Edward Albee's "Seascape" on Broadway and "Long Day's Journey Into Night" in Los Angeles. Her last movie role was in *The Assam Garden* in 1985.

In 1997 Deborah Kerr was made a Commander of the Order of British Empire, or CBE, by Queen Elizabeth II.

Regarding her personal life, in 1945 Kerr married Anthony Charles Bartley, whom she had met when he was a squadron leader in the Royal Air Force. They had two daughters, and divorced in 1959. A year later, she married Peter Viertel, a novelist/screenwriter, with whom she lived on a large estate with two trout ponds in the Swiss Alpine resort of Klosters and in a villa in Marbella, Spain. Kerr later returned to England as her health worsened.

Deborah Kerr passed away from complications from Parkinson's disease on October 16, 2007 in Suffolk, England at the age of 86.

Awards

Deborah Kerr was nominated six times for the Best Actress Academy Award - for *Edward, My Son* (1949), *From Here to Eternity* (1953), *The King and I* (1956), *Heaven Knows, Mr. Allison* (1957), *Separate Tables* (1958), *and The Sundowners* (1960).She never won an Oscar, but in 1993 she received an honorary Oscar for her contribution to the film industry. The citation called her "an artist of impeccable grace and beauty, a

---

74 On the other hand, someone like Marilyn Monroe, who was very talented, drove directors crazy by not showing up on time, not being prepared, etc.

75 From a CBS News obituary on Deborah Kerr on the day after she died.

dedicated actress whose motion picture career has always stood for perfection, discipline and elegance."

She won a Golden Globe award for Best Actress - Comedy or Musical for *The King and I* in 1957. Kerr was also nominated for Golden Globes for *Edward, My Son, Heaven Knows, Mr. Allison,* and *Separate Tables.* She was also nominated for a Primetime Emmy Award in 1985 for Outstanding Supporting Actress in a Limited Series or a Special for *A Woman of Substance.*

Kerr was also nominated for four BAFTA awards and was a 1985 Cannes Film Festival recipient for her overall body of work. Well deserved!

My Favorite Deborah Kerr Films

There are three Deborah Kerr films that stand out from the rest. I have also added four others that I really like. As always, these are my favorite films of that forgotten star, which may not necessarily be their best films.

1. *From Here to Eternity* - 1953
2. *The King and I* - 1956
3. *An Affair To Remember* - 1957
4. *Julius Caesar* - 1951
5. *Quo Vadis* - 1951
6. *The Prisoner of Zenda* - 1952
7. *King Solomon's Mines* - 1950

1. *From Here to Eternity* - 1953

From Here to Eternity is the story of three soldiers (Burt Lancaster, Montgomery Clift, and Frank Sinatra) on the island of Oahu just before, during, and after the bombing of Pearl Harbor on December 7, 1941.

Sometime in early 1941, Robert E. Lee Prewitt (Montgomery Clift) requests an Army transfer and ends up at Schofield Barracks in Hawaii. His new captain, Dana Holmes, has heard of his boxing prowess and is keen to get him to represent the company. However, Prewitt is adamant that he doesn't want to box anymore, so Captain Holmes gets his subordinates to make his life a living hell until he agrees to get in the ring. Meanwhile, Sergeant Milton Warden (Burt Lancaster) starts seeing the captain's wife, Karen Holmes (Deborah Kerr), who has a history of seeking "outside satisfaction" from a troubled marriage. Prewitt's friend Angelo Maggio (Frank Sinatra) has a few altercations with the sadistic stockade Sergeant "Fatso" Judson (Ernest Borgnine in a very brutal role), and Prewitt begins falling in love with social club employee Lorene (Donna Reed). Unbeknownst to anyone at the time, the attack on Pearl Harbor is just about to take place; when it does, it changes the lives of everyone.

Of course, the most famous scene in the movie is the one of Burt Lancaster and Deborah Kerr making love on the beach. However, the entire film is worth mentioning as one of the best in the history of American films. Lancaster, Kerr, and Clift head the all-star cast, but Sinatra and Reed won Best Supporting Actor and Actress Oscars for their work. *From Here to Eternity* won eight Oscars, including Best Picture and Best Director. It had a budget of $1.6 million but grossed $30 million, so the film was a huge commercial and critical success. And in 2002, *From Here to Eternity* was selected for preservation in the National Film Registry by the Library of Congress as being "culturally, historically, or aesthetically significant."

Ernest Borgnine, Burt Lancaster, and Frank Sinatra in a scene from *From Here to Eternity*. This was the film that actually restarted Frank Sinatra's career. And he was terrific in the film.

2. The King and I- 1956

The King and I was truly one of the great Richard Rodgers/Oscar Hammerstein musicals. When it was brought from the Broadway stage to the big screen, Deborah Kerr played the role of Anna Leonowens, the widow who accepts the role of governess to the King of Siam (Yul Brynner) to educate his children as he attempts to modernize his backward country.

Mrs. Anna Leonowens and her son Louis arrive in Bangkok, Siam (present day Thailand), where she has been contracted to teach English to the children of the royal household. She threatens to leave when the house she had been promised is not available, but falls in love with the children. A new slave, Tuptim (Rita Moreno), a gift of a vassal king, translates *Uncle Tom's Cabin* into a Siamese ballet. After expressing her unhappiness at being with the King, the slave decides to attempt to escape with her lover, a plan that does not work at all. Anna and the King start to fall in love, but her headstrong upbringing inhibits her from joining his harem. Will she stay or will she go back to England?

The King and I is a great film, with an outstanding cast led by Oscar winner Yul Brynner and Oscar nominee Deborah Kerr, great direction, and those terrific Rodgers and Hammerstein songs. It also demonstrates the growth of a king who starts out set in his ways but makes major changes in his life. The film won five Oscars and was nominated for four more. It cost $4.5 million to make and grossed over $21 million. By the way, Deborah Kerr's songs were dubbed by Marni Nixon.

> Marni Nixon also did the voices of Maria in *West Side Story* and Eliza Doolittle in *My Fair Lady*. She also played one of the singing nuns in *The Sound of Music*.

3. An Affair to Remember - 1957

This was always my mother's favorite movie and the favorite film of lots of other women also. If you don't believe me, just watch the film *Sleepless in Seattle*, which pays homage to this film.

An Affair to Remember stars Cary Grant and Deborah Kerr as passengers on an ocean liner from London to New York City who meet and fall in love. Playboy painter Nickie Ferrante's (Cary Grant at his suave very best) return to New York to marry a rich heiress is well publicized by all the major media and news organizations. During the voyage, he meets a nightclub singer, Terry McKay, (Deborah Kerr) who is also on her way home to her longtime boyfriend (Richard Denning). At first, she sees Ferrante as just another playboy and he sees her as stand-offish but over several days they soon find they've fallen in love.

Nickie has never really worked in his life - he is an artist, a painter - so they agree that they will meet again in exactly six months atop the Empire State building. This will give them time to deal with their current relationships and for Nickie to see if he can actually earn a living. He returns to painting and is reasonably successful. On the agreed date, Nickie is waiting patiently for Terry who is racing to join him. Fate intervenes however resulting in misunderstanding and heartbreak but only temporarily.

An Affair to Remember is one of the great romance movies of all time. And the ending is something special. If you don't get choked up or get a tear in your eye in the last scene of the film, there is probably something wrong with you. And the performances of both Cary Grant and Deborah Kerr are something special to remember. The film has often been duplicated (see the version with Warren Beatty) but never equaled. Not even by Tom Hanks and Meg Ryan!

4. *Julius Caesar* - 1951

This is a faithful rendering of the classic Shakespeare play about the assassination of Julius Caesar by Brutus, Cassius, and the other conspirators, and the aftermath of that assassination and how their devoted Roman followers suddenly turned on them after Marc Antony's famous "Friends, Romans, countrymen, lend me your ears" speech. Deborah Kerr plays Portia, the devoted wife of Brutus, who is very concerned about his welfare during the plot to kill Caesar but remains the dutiful wife without asking too many questions.

The film features an all-star cast that includes James Mason as Brutus and John Gielgud as Cassius, the chief conspirators; Edmond O'Brien as another plotter, Casca; Louis Calhern as Julius Caesar, Greer Garson as Caesar's wife Calpurnia, and Marlon Brando, outstanding in the role of Marc Antony. It was directed by Joseph Mankiewicz and won an Oscar for Best Art Direction but was nominated for four others, including Best Picture and Marlon Brando for Best Actor. It was not a huge commercial success, however, breaking about even. About the only criticism of the film is that it is a bit stagy, but after all, it was based on a play by Williams Shakespeare.

> The great nephew of Joseph Mankiewicz is Ben Mankiewicz, the current host of Turner Classic Movies, who replaced Robert Osborne after the death of the latter. I met Osborne once at a lecture. When I asked him who were his favorite male and female classic film stars, he said Cary Grant for the male (not surprising) and Gene Tierney (surprising, but I liked his choice) as his favorite female star.

Gene Tierney, perhaps the most beautiful movie star ever.She was Laura, in the film of the same name, among her hits.

5. *Quo Vadis* - 1951

I also like biblical spectacle-type movies, and *Quo Vadis* is one of the best. Robert Taylor and Deborah Kerr are the two stars of the film, and they are excellent together.

Returning to Rome after three years in the field, General Marcus Vinicius (Robert Taylor as a loyal Roman who has a general disdain for Christians - he really can't figure out what makes them tick) meets a devout Christian woman, Lygia (Deborah Kerr) and falls in love with her, though as a Christian she wants nothing to do with a Roman soldier. While she grew up Roman, the adopted daughter of a retired general, Lygia is technically a ward of Rome. Marcus gets Emperor Nero (Peter Ustinov, who makes a great Nero) to give her to him for his great service to Rome, but finds himself succumbing gradually to her Christian faith. The cast also includes Leo Genn as Petronius, the wise advisor to Nero, and Finley Currie as the apostle Peter.

Quo Vadis was a true MGM spectacular, running almost three hours in length and in beautiful color. It was nominated for eight Academy Awards, including both Peter Ustinov and Leo Genn for Best Supporting Actor, and Best Picture. While it did not win any Oscars, Ustinov won a Golden Globe Award for Best Supporting Actor. And while its cost was only around $7 million, it earned around $45 million, a very nice total for 1951.

> The term "Quo Vadis" actually means "Where are you going?" It was basically a command that Jesus gave to Peter to return to Rome to continue his ministry.

6. and 7. *Prisoner of Zenda* (1952) and *King Solomon's Mines* (1950)

These two movies have already been discussed under the films of Stewart Granger. Deborah Kerr was the leading lady in both of those films.

Deborah Kerr was certainly an excellent actress. Her six Best Actress nominations tell you that much.Often playing cool and aloof women, she was also good in adventure films, comedies, dramas, and biblical spectacles. She played opposite the most popular male stars of that era, and always held her own.

14. Robert Montgomery (1904-1981)

Robert Montgomery was one of those very few actors who also excelled at directing. His long career lasted from the late 1920s to the early 1960s. Montgomery was also a Naval hero in World War II, an advisor to President Eisenhower, and the father of actress Elizabeth Montgomery (*Bewitched*). He also produced a popular television show, *Robert Montgomery Presents*, from 1950 to 1957.

Biography

Robert Montgomery was born Henry Montgomery Jr. on May 21, 1904 in Beacon, N.Y. His father was a vice president of the New York Rubber Company. Robert received his early education at the Pawling

(N.Y.) School and studied in Europe. When his father died and it was discovered that the family fortune had vanished, Robert went to work as a mechanic's helper in a railroad yard. Later, he worked as a wiper in the engine room of an oil tanker and tried his hand at writing short stories and plays - interesting combination! They were never published or produced. But as you can see, he did not grow up with a silver spoon in his mouth.

The plays, however, led him to the stage, and in September 1924, he made his Broadway debut playing a butler, a valet, a guest and an off-stage voice in William Faversham's "The Mask and the Face." He played stock performances and had roles in several Broadway plays. One, "The Possession," brought him an MGM contract and a minor part in the film *So This Is College*. A good role in *The Big House* in 1930 as a weak playboy who turns informer in prison helped assure Montgomery's success in the new medium of talking films.

He was soon playing opposite some of Hollywood's biggest female stars, including Greta Garbo in *Inspiration,* Norma Shearer in *The Divorcee,* Myrna Loy in *Petticoat Fever* (as opposed to *Petticoat Junction*), Joan Crawford in *The Last of Mrs. Cheyney* and Helen Hayes in *Vanessa.* He also appeared with Irene Dunne, Carole Lombard, Bette Davis, Susan Hayward, and Ingrid Bergman.

During his screen-acting days, Mr. Montgomery gained a reputation as one of Hollywood's wittiest conversationalists, with a flair for the acid remark. Once, speaking of the owner of a trade newspaper who demanded "good will" advertisements from actors in payment for printing favorable comments about them - or panning them if they did not buy the advertisements - Mr. Montgomery said, "The secret of his success lies in the fact that he refuses to stay bought. He makes his victims buy him on the installment plan."

Another delight of Mr. Montgomery was deflating pretentiousness. He once described the oversized living room of a Beverly Hills colonial "cottage" as a "knotty-pine indoor tennis court."

Eventually Montgomery also got into directing. His first directing opportunity came when John Ford, a fellow officer in the Navy, broke his leg during the production of *They Were Expendable*, a patriotic film about PT boats made during the last days of World War II that also included John Wayne in the cast. Montgomery took over directing of the final scenes.

The film's success earned Mr. Montgomery a chance to direct a Raymond Chandler melodrama, *Lady in the Lake*, in 1946. He also played the leading role as detective Philip Marlowe[76], but attracted attention by photographing the entire action as a "first person" film, seen through the detective's eyes. Mr. Montgomery was visible only once, when the camera looked at his reflection in a mirror. After that, Robert Montgomery directed such films as *Ride the Pink Horse, Once More, My Darling* and *The Gallant Hours,* a biography of the late Adm. William F. Halsey Jr., starring his old friend James Cagney.

Montgomery also worked as a director on the Broadway stage, most notably on "The Desperate Hours" and the 1962 success "Calculated Risk," starring Joseph Cotten. He was an advisor to President Dwight Eisenhower on how to do public speaking before a television audience, and actually had an office in the White House.

In his later years, he kept himself occupied with lectures and dramatic readings, but was also busy with his farm in Canaan Valley, Connecticut. "You're talking to a farmer," he told an interviewer once. "I've just come in from fertilizing the fields for the coming year."

Mr. Montgomery's first marriage in 1928 to the actress Elizabeth Allen ended in divorce. He was survived by his second wife, the former Elizabeth Grant Harkness, and two children by his first marriage, Robert and Elizabeth Montgomery, the actress.

Awards

---

76 Lots of actors have played Philip Marlowe on the big screen, including Humphrey Bogart, Dick Powell, Robert Mitchum, James Garner, Robert Montgomery, George Montgomery (no relation), and Elliot Gould. Humphrey Bogart is the most famous, but Dick Powell might actually have done the best job in 1944's *Murder, My Sweet.*

Robert Montgomery was nominated for two Best Actor Academy Awards. In 1938, he was nominated for *Night Must Fall*, but lost out to Spencer Tracy in *Captains Courageous*. In 1942 he was nominated for *Here Comes Mr. Jordan* but lost out to Gary Cooper in *Sergeant York* (Montgomery was good, but Cooper was terrific as the reluctant World War I hero, Alvin York.)

My Favorite Robert Montgomery Films include:

1. *Here Comes Mr. Jordan* - 1941
2. *Lady in the Lake* - 1946 (also directed the film)
3. *They Were Expendable* - 1945
4. *Night Must Fall* - 1937
5. *The Gallant Hours* - 1960 (as director only)

1. *Here Comes Mr. Jordan* - 1941

Here Comes Mr. Jordan is one of my favorite comedy/fantasy movies, and Robert Montgomery is the star of the film (although Claude Rains is Mr. Jordan.) Montgomery plays a professional boxer who is also a saxophone player and flies his own private plane. One day Joe Pendleton (Montgomery) is flying his plane to his next fight, when the plane suddenly crashes. However, his spirit is pulled from the plane by a Heavenly Messenger, new on the job. Unfortunately, we learn that upon further review by Heaven, Joe would have survived the crash and actually lived another 50 years! But his body has already been cremated, so he can't just go back to his old body.

Well, a senior heavenly official - Claude Rains as Mr. Jordan - has to step in and find Joe another body. He finds one in the person of wealthy Bruce Farnsworth, a wealthy but unscrupulous businessman who has just been murdered by his wife and her boyfriend. So Joe sets out to do two things as Farnsworth - 1) make him a better, more honest person, and 2) make him into a professional boxer so that Joe can fight again in Farnsworth's body. To the moviegoer, he still looks like Joe Pendleton, but to the actors in the film, he looks like Farnsworth. [77]

77 That's how the movie gets away with having Montgomery play a double role of two guys who don't really resemble each other.

152

This outstanding film is funny, very touching, and has a moral point to make. And again, if you don't get a tear in your eye with this ending and get choked up, there is something wrong with you. A truly great cast includes Edward Everett Horton as the Heavenly Messenger, Evelyn Keyes as the girl that Farnsworth falls in love with (whose father had been the victim of one of the pre-Robert Montgomery Farnsworth's dishonest business deals), James Gleason as the befuddled boxer's manager, and Rita Johnson and John Emery as Farnsworth's wife and her lover.

The film won two Oscars for best original writing and best screenplay, and was nominated for five others, including Best Picture, Best Actor (Montgomery), Best Supporting Actor (James Gleason), and Best Director (Alexander Hall).

> If I ever do a book about supporting actors, Claude Rains will probably be the first one in it. What a terrific actor he was!

Claude Rains. Yes, he was in *Casablanca*, but he also made so many other great films.

2. *Lady in the Lake* - 1946

What makes this film so different is that the leading man (Robert Montgomery) is also the camera for the movie.We only see his face once - when he is looking in a mirror - aside from when he directly addresses the audience a couple of times.

Montgomery plays private detective Philip Marlowe, who is hired by a female executive of a publishing firm to find the publisher's wife, who is supposed to have run off to Mexico. But the guy she was supposed to have run off with says he has not seen the woman in two months. And the case soon becomes much more complicated as several people are murdered and the double crosses mount. Let's just say it's hard to tell the good guys and gals from the baddies.

Robert Montgomery does a good job in serving as both the director and leading man. And the stellar supporting cast includes Audrey Totter, who is really good as the female executive of the publishing firm, Leon Ames as the publisher, plus Lloyd Nolan as a brutal policeman who gives Marlowe a tough time all the time, Tom Tully, and Jayne Meadows, who was the wife of Steve Allen in real life.

Here's Jayne Meadows, pointing a guy at Philip Marlowe in this film.Her sister was Audrey Meadows, who played Alice Kramden in *The Honeymooners* with Jackie Gleason.

3. *They Were Expendable* - 1945

In the wake of Pearl Harbor's surprise attack by the Japanese on December 7, 1941, Lt. John Brickley's (Robert Montgomery) experimental squadron of agile fast-attack Patrol Torpedo boats is sent to hot and humid Manila to avert a potentially imminent Japanese invasion. As he and his second-in-command, Lieutenant "Rusty" Ryan (John Wayne), desperately try to prove the newly-founded naval unit's worth, the enemy launches a devastating all-out attack; and despite the PT boat flotilla's undeniable success, the considerably outnumbered and outgunned American soldiers are fighting a losing battle.

Little by little, the Philippine campaign is doomed to cave in, as comrades-in-arms perish in the sea. But the PT boats continue to do their best, and give U.S. forces the time to build up, because, after all, "They were expendable."

It is interesting to note that during production, John Ford had put John Wayne down every chance he got, because Wayne had not enlisted to fight in World War II - he was exempt for family issues. Ford commanded a naval photographic unit during the war, rising to the rank of captain and thought Wayne a coward for staying behind. After months of Ford heaping insults on Wayne's head, co-star Robert Montgomery finally approached the director and told him that if he was putting Wayne down for Montgomery's benefit (Montgomery had also served as a naval officer in the war, as a skipper of a PT boat), then he needed to stop immediately. This brought the tough-as-nails director to tears and he stopped abusing Wayne.[78]

Montgomery actually helped direct some of the PT sequences for the film when John Ford broke his leg three weeks into filming.(He certainly had the experience for that!). Montgomery finished the film and was complimented by Ford for his work. Ford claimed he couldn't tell the difference between his footage and Montgomery's, who took no screen credit as an assistant director.

Donna Reed, Ward Bond, Marshall Thompson, Leon Ames, and Cameron Mitchell co-starred in this very good WWII war film.

---

78   International movie data base (IMDB)

The name of Leon Ames has appeared in the last two films. He is probably best known as Judy Garland's father in *Meet Me in St. Louis.*

Character actor Leon Ames had over 150 film credits and alsoreceived a Screen Actors Guild Lifetime Achievement Award.

4. *Night Must Fall* - 1937

In a small English village, the police drag the river, searching for the body of Mrs. Shellbrook, who has been missing for several days. Meanwhile, grumpy old Mrs. Bransom (Dame May Whitty) hires a charming young man named Danny (Robert Montgomery) as a live-in companion/handyman. Less charmed by Danny is Mrs. Bransom's niece, Olivia (Rosalind Russell, way before she was Auntie Mame), a repressed young woman who suspects Danny of foul play. When news of a local murder is revealed, Olivia suspects Danny. Although repulsed by the thought he may have committed the crime, Olivia also finds herself becoming increasingly attracted to him at the same time. Others things happen, which makes Olivia more and more convinced that Danny is in fact the murderer.

One of the few times in his career when Robert Montgomery was the villain, and he makes the most of it as a creepy killer. This was his first of two Best Actor Oscar nominations, and as I have indicated, he lost out to Spencer Tracy. But this is an impressive relatively early film for Montgomery. *Night Must Fall* was based on a stage play by Emlyn Williams; the movie achieved critical but not financial success.

5. *The Gallant Hours* - 1960

Night Must Fall was another foray into directing by Robert Montgomery. A semi-documentary dramatization of five weeks in the life of Vice Admiral William F. "Bull" Halsey, Jr. (played with passion by James Cagney), from his assignment to command the U.S. naval operations in the South Pacific to the Allied victory at Guadalcanal.

Night Must Fall is told in a more narrative style than most documentaries, but it works. Dennis Weaver and Richard Jaeckel are among the co-stars in this WWII film.

Robert Montgomery was one of those rare Hollywood stars of that era who also ventured into producing and directing. And how many actors can say they coached the President of the United States on how to deliver television speeches?

He was also a pretty normal, down-to-earth guy. You can tell that by this quote: "If you are lucky enough to be a success, by all means enjoy the applause and the adulation of the public. But never, never believe it." I am guessing he was never full of himself like a lot of stars.

15. Rita Hayworth (1918-1987)

The best one-word description of Rita Hayworth would be glamorous. One of the most popular female movie stars of the 1940s and 1950s, her nickname was "The Love Goddess," and she was married five times, including to an Arabian prince. Unlike some of the Hollywood glamour girls of that era, she was also an excellent dancer, good enough to share the stage with both Fred Astaire and Gene Kelly.[79] The star of 65 films, at the end of her life, she was one of those celebrities who raised awareness of Alzheimer's disease because of her personal struggle with the disease.

---

79 I liked Fred Astaire, a very graceful dancer, but he was too much of a ballroom dancer for me. I always preferred Gene Kelly, powerful and athletic and generally in slacks and a t-shirt.

Biography

Rita Hayworth was born in New York City, on Oct. 17, 1918. Her father, Eduardo Cansino, was a Spanish-born dancer and her mother, the former Volga Haworth, had been a Ziegfeld Follies showgirl. They named their daughter Margarita Carmen Cansino, but she shortened the name to Rita Cansino when she began dancing professionally at the age of 12, and kept that name for her first 10 movies.

Mr. Cansino's career took the family to Los Angeles, where his daughter attended school through the ninth grade. Then she joined her father's act and performed in clubs in Tijuana and Agua Caliente, Mexico, where, when she was 16 years old, she was spotted by a Fox Film Company producer, who signed her to a contract.

Making her film debut in 1935 in *Under the Pampas Moon*, Rita Cansino appeared in a succession of lesser roles, such as that of a dance hall girl in a Spencer Tracy movie called *Dante's Inferno*. Other films in her Cansino period included *Charlie Chan in Egypt*, *Human Cargo*, and *Meet Nero Wolfe*, with Edward Arnold as the famous detective.

The Fox company's merger with 20th-Century Pictures left Rita without a contract, but in 1937 she met and married the man who was to become her manager and dramatically change her career fortunes. He was Edward Judson, a shrewd businessman 22 years her senior, under whose guidance she had her eyebrows and hairline altered by electrolysis, and was transformed from a raven-haired Latin to an auburn-haired Anglo-Saxon. Judson also changed his wife's professional name, choosing her mother's maiden name of Haworth and adding a "y" to clarify the pronunciation. He hired press agents to get the name and picture of Rita Hayworth into newspapers and fan magazines, and ultimately won her a seven-year contract at Columbia Pictures.

But low-budget B movies continued to be Rita's fate, except for the 1939 *Only Angels Have Wings*, with Cary Grant, in which the director, Howard Hawks, cast her as an unfaithful wife. It was the secondary female role, but one that got the actress her first good critical notices.

At that time, a *Life* magazine writer dubbed her "The Love Goddess," which stuck with her for the rest of her career.

Beginning in 1941, Miss Hayworth rapidly developed into one of the biggest female stars in Hollywood. On loan to Warner Brothers, Hayworth appeared opposite James Cagney in *Strawberry Blonde* in 1941 and, back at Columbia, she achieved full star status when she was cast as Mr. Astaire's dancing partner in *You'll Never Get Rich*, a 1941 hit that got her a *Time* magazine cover article and instant celebrity status. In 1942, she appeared in three hit movies, including another one with Fred Astaire and another with Victor Mature.

Rita Hayworth, unlike stars who claimed to deplore their own publicity, reveled in hers. "Why should I mind?" she said. "I like having my picture taken and being a glamorous person. Sometimes when I find myself getting impatient, I just remember the times I cried my eyes out because nobody wanted to take my picture at the Trocadero."[80]

After that came *Gilda*, which ran into censorship trouble in some areas because of the so-called strip scene. In it, she wore a clinging black satin strapless gown and, while coyly peeling off long black gloves, sang a mildly suggestive song called "Put the Blame on Mame."

Hayworth, who had divorced her first husband, married director/actor Orson Welles in 1943, and they had a daughter, Rebecca. While Mr. Welles was directing her in one of her best films, *The Lady From Shanghai* (1949), she filed for divorce from him. Miss Hayworth had met and fallen in love with Prince Aly Khan and, since neither was divorced at the time, their travels together through Europe provoked some public indignation.

When they were married in 1949, the fact that Miss Hayworth was visibly pregnant was widely reported. She divorced Aly Khan two years later and was subsequently married to and divorced from the singer Dick Haymes and then James Hill, a movie producer. I think that makes a total of five altogether. She was in other movies in the 50s and 60s, including *Salome* with Stewart Granger and *Pal Joey* with Frank Sinatra but gradually moved away from the big screen after that.

---

80 *New York Times* obituary

Rita Hayworth attempted a stage career in 1971, but it ended abruptly because she was unable to remember her lines. Six years later, a court in Santa Ana, Calif., named an administrator for her affairs on the recommendation of a physician who said she was disabled by chronic alcoholism. Despite her heavy drinking, however, it later appeared that the diagnosis of alcoholism might have been only part of the problem, and that Miss Hayworth was also actually suffering from the first stages of Alzheimer's disease.

In June 1981, a court in Los Angeles declared the actress legally unable to care for herself, and she was put in the care of her daughter Princess Yasmin, who took her to New York to live. Princess Yasmin, testifying in 1983 before a Congressional committee concerned with appropriating funds for Alzheimer's disease research, said that the disease had reduced her mother to "a state of utter helplessness." The Princess subsequently became a spokesperson on Alzheimer's Disease and dementia.[81]

Rita Hayworth passed away on May 14, 1987 in New York City at age 68. Then-President Ronald Reagan, a close friend, said "Rita Hayworth was one of our country's most beloved stars. Glamorous and talented, she gave us many wonderful moments on the stage and screen and delighted audiences from the time she was a young girl. Nancy and I are saddened by Rita's death. She was a friend whom we will miss."

Awards

Rita Hayworth was nominated for a Golden Globe for Best Actress for *Circus World* in 1965 but did not win. Frankly, it was not really one of her best films, although any movie with John Wayne and Rita Hayworth in it can't be all that bad.

My Favorite Rita Hayworth Films

It was fairly easy for me to select the following as my favorite Rita Hayworth films:

---

81 She served on the Board of Directors of several Alzheimers-related organizations and charities.

1. *Gilda* - 1946
2. *Cover Girl* - 1944
3. *The Lady from Shanghai* - 1947
4. *Blood and Sand* - 1941
5. *Pal Joey* - 1957
6. *They Came to Cordura* - 1959

1. *Gilda* - 1946

If you want to see one movie that clearly demonstrates the sex appeal of Rita Hayworth, *Gilda* would be that film. She clearly establishes herself as the ultimate femme fatale in this drama/film noir. I can still see her singing "Put the Blame on Mame" whenever I think of this flick, and that is not even her voice singing that song.[82]

Johnny Farrell (Glenn Ford) is a small-time American gambler, newly arrived in Buenos Aires, Argentina. When he is caught cheating at a game of blackjack, Farrell manages to talk his way into a job with the casino's owner, the powerful Ballin Mundson (George Macready in a really mean and nasty role). The two form an uneasy partnership based off their mutual lack of scruples until Mundson introduces Farrell to his beautiful new wife, Gilda (Rita Hayworth), who just happens to be Farrell's ex-lover. A lot of trouble brews after that, and the question is who will still be alive by the end of the film?

Glenn Ford is really good as the protagonist, George Macready is at his nastiest as the casino owner, and Rita Hayworth is drop-dead gorgeous as the title figure, Gilda; she also gives a very good performance, as most of the plot twists seem to center around her.

Supposedly, the character of Jessica Rabbit in the 1988 live-action plus animation hit, *Who Framed Roger Rabbit*, is based on Rita Hayworth in *Gilda*. And I believe it.

---

82 That was actually Anita Ellis singing the song during the performance, although it was Rita Hayworth doing the singing at the bar when she was strumming her guitar. Columbia Pictures chief Harry Cohn never thought Rita's voice was good enough to carry a song such as this one.

Rita Hayworth

Jessica Rabbit

Directed by Charles Vidor, *Gilda* was a nominee for the Grand Prize at the 1946 Cannes Film Festival. It was honored by the National Film Registry for its importance to film in 2013.

2. *Cover Girl* - 1944

I have mentioned that Rita Hayworth was not that much of a singer, but she was a very good dancer. The fact that she danced with BOTH

Gene Kelly and Fred Astaire, and danced very well with them, says it all.

Cover Girl has a nice plot about Rusty Parker (Rita Hayworth) who dreams of being a dancer on Broadway, which means she would have to leave the small dinner theater where she works with Danny (Gene Kelly) and Genius (Phil Silvers). Rusty is in love with Danny. All three are good friends and every Friday night they go to a local bar where they get oysters so they can look for a pearl (they never eat them).

Soon Rusty enters a contest to be a "Cover Girl" as a stepping-stone in her career. She reminds the *Cover Girl* magazine publisher, John Coudair (Otto Kruger), of his lost love, showgirl Maribelle Hicks. He was engaged to Maribelle, although his wealthy society mother made fun of her. Maribelle left John at the altar when she saw the piano at her wedding. It reminded her of the piano-player she truly loved.

Rusty is actually Maribelle's granddaughter, and there are flashback musical sequences with Maribelle dancing to songs from the beginning of the 20th century. Rusty lands on the cover of her grandmother's former fiancé's magazine (as a bride). She is pursued by Coudair's pal, the wealthy theatrical producer, Noel Wheaton (Lee Bowman). He produces a lavish musical to star Rusty, surrounded by real cover girls of the mid 1940's. While Rusty does not want to leave the nightclub act with Danny, he realizes what a good opportunity it would be for her, so her pushes her away. Will Rusty end up with Wheaton or Danny? Remember, this is Gene Kelly!

The story line provides numerous opportunities for songs and dancing. And it has two questions that Rusty must answer: Is fame all that it is cracked up to be? And, Is less really more if you are happy? Those questions are the theme of the movie. The movie also does a good job of showcasing the talents of all three principal stars, including Phil Silvers' flare for comedy.

Another film directed by Charles Vidor, *Cover Girl* won an Oscar for Best Musical Score for Carmen Dragon and Morris Stoloff. If the name of orchestra leader Carmen Dragon sounds familiar, his son, Daryl

Dragon, is the Captain in the Captain and Tennille musical duo. The film was nominated for four other Oscars but lost out in all of them.

3. *The Lady From Shanghai* - 1947

In most of Orson Welles' films, it doesn't matter what the film is about. You just sit back and enjoy his camera mastery and shadow-drenched imagery. And *The Lady from Shanghai* is probably no exception. Actually, the story, based on a novel by Sherwood King, makes perfect sense after two or three viewings. Welles plays an Irish-American sailor named Michael O'Hara, who rescues a beautiful blonde from muggers in Central Park. The blonde (Elsa Bannister) is portrayed by the otherwise redheaded Rita Hayworth, who under the direction of her ex-husband Welles, delivers one of her most impressive screen performances.

The two meet again when Welles is hired on as a crew member of the yacht owned by Rita's husband, the brilliant, but physically challenged defense attorney Arthur Bannister (Everett Sloane, in an outstanding performance). As he falls deeper under Rita's spell, Welles gets involved in a bizarre insurance scam. Glenn Anders, Sloane's eccentric law partner, plans to stage his own death, collect the insurance, and skip town. All Welles has to do is pretend to murder Anders, and he'll get a big chunk of the money. As it turns out, Anders is murdered for real.

The innocent Welles is defended in court by Sloane, who is famous for never losing a case, but who in this instance seems bound and determined to lose. As the jury files out, Welles makes a break for it. Rita catches up with him at a Chinese theatre, then stands by with a glazed expression on her face as she watches her cohorts drug Welles. As he comes to in an amusement park fun house, he begins to piece the plot together; he has been set up as a clay pigeon by Rita and Sloane. Only now, Rita intends to double-cross her husband. The plot comes to a literally smashing climax in the famous "hall of mirrors" sequence.

A blonde Rita Hayworth in the classic Hall of Mirrors scene in *The Lady from Shanghai*.

4. *Blood and Sand* - 1941

A fairly early starring role for Rita Hayworth in a remake of the 1922 Rudolph Valentino hit. Uneducated peasant Juan Gallardo (Tyrone Power) rises to fame and fortune in the bullfight arena. He uses his stardom (and money) to help his impoverished family. Everything is looking good until he falls for socialite Dona Sol (Rita Hayworth); thus breaking the heart of his childhood sweetheart and wife Carmen (Linda Darnell). Nevertheless Carmen stands true to Gallardo as he continues to face danger in the bullring. He neglects his wife in favor of his new lavish and decadent life style. In other words, he gets too big for his tights. But he is brought back to earth in the bullring in a crashing finale.

Tyrone Power as Juan Gallardo is very good, as are both Rita Hayworth and Linda Darnell. A really good supporting cast includes Anthony Quinn, Laird Cregar, J. Carrol Naish, and John Carradine. The film's lavish Technicolor production helped it win a well-deserved Oscar for Best Cinematography.

Tyrone Power played all sorts of swashbuckling heroes in most of his films, including *The Mark of Zorro*, *The Black Swan*, *Captain from Castillo*, *The Black Rose*, and *Son of Fury*. It was only later in his career when he got better roles such as *Witness for the Prosecution*, *The Sun Also Rises*, *The*

Razor's Edge, and *Nightmare Alley*, perhaps his best role. He was just coming into his own as an actor when, sadly, he died of a heart attack at the young age of 44. He may have been the handsomest leading man in the history of American films; if not, he is certainly in the team photo.

Tyrone Power, a great leading man who died much too early at the age of 44.[83]

5. *Pal Joey* - 1957

Pal Joey is a 1957 film based on the 1940 play and book with music and lyrics by Richard Rodgers and Lorenz Hart. In the Broadway stage play, Joey was played by Gene Kelly; the 1957 film version featured Frank Sinatra in the title role, both very good choices.

Joey Evans is charming, handsome, funny, talented, and also a jerk. He is the emcee at a local nightclub with aspirations of owning his own club. When Joey meets the former chorus girl ("She used to be 'Vera...with the Vanishing Veils'") and now rich widow Vera Simpson (Rita Hayworth), the two big egos seem made for each other. That is,

---

83   His father, Tyrone Power, Sr. was also an actor and also died of a massive heart attack at age 62 in the arms of his son.

until Linda English (Kim Novak) comes along. Linda is a "mouse on the chorus line" and "built like there's no tomorrow." But she's the typical good little girl from a good little home -- just the right ingredient to louse up Joey's cushy set up with Vera. And of course, that is exactly what happens.

Frankly, the plot of *Pal Joey* is not all that great, but the music is terrific, with many memorable songs including "Bewitched, Bothered and Bewildered,""I Could Write a Book,""The Lady is a Tramp," There's a Small Hotel," and "I Didn't Know What Time It Was"[84]. Frank Sinatra was born to play this part, and an older Rita Hayworth (39 when the film was released) is perfect in the part of the rich and spoiled socialite widow who always gets what she wants - except perhaps not Joey Evans. *Pal Joey* was nominated for four Academy Awards but did not win any, but Frank Sinatra won a Golden Globe as Best Actor in a comedy or musical.

Frank Sinatra and Rita Hayworth in *Pal Joey*

6. *They Came to Cordura* - 1957

I chose this film because it is a pretty decent Western and an unusual film genre for Rita Hayworth.

---

84 The last three songs were in the film but not the original Broadway production, but were written by Rodgers and Hart, of course.

Gary Cooper stars in one of his final roles in *They Came To Cordura*, Robert Rossen's moody study of the thin dividing line between heroism and cowardice. Cooper plays Major Thomas Thorn, a U.S. Army officer in the expedition into Mexico against Pancho Villa in 1916. Because he hesitated during a moment of decision in a battle, he has been labeled a coward. His commanding officer, Colonel Rogers (Robert Keith), orders Thorn to recommend five men for nomination for the Congressional Medal of Honor for bravery in the battle against Villa. Angered that Thorn did not nominate him for the Medal of Honor, Rogers charges Thorn with transporting the men through a broiling and dangerous desert to the town of Cordura.

They begin the trek accompanied by Adelaide Geary (Rita Hayworth), the daughter of a dishonored U.S. Senator, who is accused of treason since she owned the hacienda where Villa's men stayed. As they travel across the desert expanse, Thorn ponders why these men are considered heroes while he is labeled a coward. As their journey continues, the heroes turn into a mutinous rabble, with Thorn reduced to holding the group at bay with a loaded gun.

They Came to Cordura has a good cast, with the five men played by Van Heflin, Tab Hunter, Richard Conte, Michael Callan, and Dick York. Rita Hayworth is virtually the only female in the entire cast. But this is basically Gary Cooper's film and provides a good examination of what really makes up heroism versus cowardice.

Though never a great actress, Rita Hayworth was a true Hollywood star and made many movies, with these six being among my favorites. But she will always be best known for *Gilda*, as far as I am concerned.

16. Joel McCrea (1905-1990)

The characteristic that I like best about Joel McCrea is that while he is best known for his Westerns - and he made a lot of them! - he also did very well in romantic comedies and dramas.

Not ridiculously handsome like a Tyrone Power, Robert Taylor, or Burt Lancaster, he had more of a typical average wholesome American aura about him than some others. And why not? After all, he was happily married to actress Frances Dee for 57 years until his death, certainly a rarity in Hollywood in that or any other era.

Before World War II, he played in a lot of romantic comedies and dramas, but after the War, he stuck mainly to his favorite film genre - the Western. And why not? He was very good in them.

As he explained it years later: "I liked doing comedies, but as I got older I was better suited to do Westerns. Because I think it becomes unattractive for an older fellow trying to look young, falling in love with attractive girls ... I always felt so much more comfortable in the Western. The minute I got a horse and a hat and a pair of boots on, I felt easier. I didn't feel like I was an actor anymore. I felt like I was the guy out there doing it."[85]

Biography

Joel McCrea was born on Nov. 5, 1905, in South Pasadena, Calif., of Scottish-Irish descent. His family moved to Hollywood when he was nine. He attended Hollywood High School and Pomona College, where he studied drama and appeared in plays.

His father, Thomas McCrea, was a utility executive. "The family was moderately well-off," the actor once told an interviewer, "but I always wanted to work and own my own things." So, from the age of nine, he was successively a home-delivery newsboy, a construction-site teamster and later a movie wrangler, stunt man and bit player. From his youth, he maintained his own horses and rode them all around town. That's probably why he was such a natural in Westerns.

He studied acting at Pomona College, which he graduated from in 1928, and got some stage experience at the Pasadena Community Playhouse, where other future stars such as Randolph Scott, Dana Andrews, Robert Young, and Victor Mature would also get their first experience. McCrea also worked as an extra and did some stunt work.

He won featured roles at the age of 23 and his first leading role at 24, in an action film, *The Silver Horde,* which brought him invaluable instruction from a co-star, Louis Wolheim.

85　From www.BestMoviesbyFarr.com, a movie fan's blog

GARY KOCA

"He taught me more in 10 weeks than I had learned in four years of college," McCrea recalled. "He used to tell me how mentally lazy I was. 'You've got to think, not act,' he'd say. 'Your face is expressive enough. When you think, I can read your thoughts. So, if you want to show you are mad, don't scowl: just think mad and you'll look mad.'"

A contract at MGM soon followed, and that was followed by a better contract at RKO. Will Rogers also took a liking to the young man (they shared a love of ranching and roping) and did much to elevate McCrea's career.His wholesome looks and quiet manner were soon in demand, primarily in romantic dramas and comedies, and he became an increasingly popular leading man in the 30s and 40s. Joel hoped to concentrate on Westerns, but several years passed before he could convince the studio heads to cast him in one.

Meanwhile, McCrea appeared in a total of 38 movies in the 1930's, smoothly alternating between action-adventure films, melodramas, dramas, romances and comedies. The films included *The Lost Squadron* (1932), *The Most Dangerous Game* (1932), *Private Worlds* (1935), *Barbary Coast* (1935), *Dead End* (1937),and *They Shall Have Music* (1939).

After World War II, he settled into western roles in such movies as *The Virginian* (1946), *Four Faces West* (1948), *Colorado Territory* (1949), *Stars in My Crown* (1950)), and *Ride the High Country* (1962). In the last film, a low-budget classic directed by Sam Peckinpah, McCrea and Randolph Scott made a great team as a pair of older, graying cowpokes.

Joel McCrea and actress Frances Dee were married for 57 years. They lived during their entire marriage in Thousand Oaks, Calif., and had three sons, Joel (Jody), David, and Peter. Jody McCrea played young leading roles in films of the late 1950's and 60's and portrayed a deputy marshal to his father in a western television series, *Wichita Town,* broadcast in 1959 and 1960.

Though born in the Los Angeles area, McCrea's family frontier roots were actually very deep. Joel McCrea's paternal grandfather, Maj. John McCrea, had been a stagecoach driver between San Bernardino and Los Angeles; his maternal grandfather, Albert Whipple, was lured to San Francisco by the 1849 gold rush. In 1985, the actor observed that all his ancestors had been frontiersmen. Noting that many of his roles were variations of them, he concluded, "That's why my heart was in it."

Throughout his life, Joel McCrea invested wisely in real estate and became a multi millionaire through real estate holdings and his movie career. A park in Thousand Oaks, California is even named in his honor.

Joel McCrea passed away on October 20, 1990 at the age of 84 of complications from pneumonia. A few weeks earlier he had appeared at a fund raiser for Republican gubernatorial candidate Pete Wilson.

Awards

While Joel McCrea never was nominated for any Oscars himself, many of his films received awards and nominations.

McCrea was a 1987 Golden Boot Award winner[86] and a 1987 Los Angeles Film Critics Association Award for career achievement. He was also a 1976 Western Heritage award winner[87] for outstanding family entertainment in a western motion picture.

My Favorite Joel McCrea Films

I have included a sample of my favorite Joel McCrea movies, which represent dramas, romantic comedies, and, of course, Westerns. As you can see, however, only two of them are really westerns.

1. *Foreign Correspondent* - 1940
2. *Sullivan's Travels* - 1941
3. *Ride the High Country* - 1962
4. *The More, the Merrier* - 1943

---

86 Award honoring actors, actresses, and crew members who have made significant contributions to the genre of Western television and movies.

87 An award honoring the legacy of men and women for their works in western literature, music, film, and television.

5. *The Palm Beach Story* - 1942
6. *The Most Dangerous Game* - 1932
7. *The Great Man's Lady* - 1942

1. *Foreign Correspondent* - 1940

This really good film directed by Alfred Hitchcock was made a year or so before America's entry into World War II but focuses on a ring of Nazi spies attempting to aid the Axis overthrow of England.

Johnny Jones (Joel McCrea)[88] is an action reporter on a New York daily newspaper. He covers local crime and other related stories. The editor (Harry Davenport) appoints him European correspondent because he is fed up with the dry, lackluster reports he currently gets from his reporters. Jones' first assignment under the pen name of Huntley Haverstock is to get the inside story on a secret treaty agreed to between two European countries by the famous diplomat, Mr. Van Meer (Albert Bassermann).

However things don't go as planned and Jones enlists the help of a young woman, Carol, (Laraine Day) to help track down a group of spies. Her father (Herbert Marshall in a good role) is a British official and head of the Universal Peace Party, which is assisting in the agreement.

Someone posing as a photographer shoots Van Meer as he exits the meeting, and Johnny grabs a car driven by Carol to follow in pursuit. They end up at a local windmill, where Johnny tries to find the shooter while Carol goes back for help. But was that really Van Meer who was shot? Johnny's life is now in danger because of what he has seen and knows. And just who are the patriots and who are the spies?

The supporting cast includes George Sanders as another reporter, who helps Johnny throughout the effort; Edmund Gwenn as the most jovial

---

88 Alfred Hitchcock originally wanted Gary Cooper for the lead, but Coop turned him down because he did not want to do a thriller. After he saw the film, Cooper told Hitchcock he made a big mistake by turning down this film. Yes, he did! But Joel McCrea was terrific!

hitman you will ever see in a movie; Robert Benchley; and Martin Kosleck (always playing a spy). I should mention that although Nazi Germany is never directly mentioned, the viewer knows who they are referring to. It is also a very patriotic work from Hitchcock regarding his native England.

This terrific thriller/spy film was nominated for six Academy Awards, including Best Picture, but did not win any. For one thing, it was up against *Rebecca* (another Hitchcock film), *The Philadelphia Story*, and *The Grapes of Wrath*. But it is an excellent thriller, very worthy of Alfred Hitchcock. Determining who is a spy and who is not results in a lot of surprises. And the climax - as a plane returning to America is shot down by an enemy destroyer with all the principals aboard the plane - is extremely exciting.

By the way, shooting was completed on May 29, 1940, after which Alfred Hitchcock made a visit to England. He returned on July 3 with the word that the Germans were expected to start bombing at any time. Ben Hecht was hurriedly called in and wrote the tacked-on final scene set at a London radio station. It was filmed on July 5, and the real-life bombing started on July 10, 1940.[89][90]

Actress Laraine Day was at one time married to baseball manager Leo Durocher for 13 years. She took such an active interest in his career and in baseball in general that she acquired the nickname "The First

---

89 IMDB notes on *Foreign Correspondent*

90 When this movie was made, America was not part of World War II. At this time, a number of Hollywood studios were pro-American involvement in the war. This movie is one of a number of films made during the late 1930s and early 1940s that represented pro-American intervention in the war. These films include *Confessions of a Nazi Spy* (1939), *The Mortal Storm* (1940), *A Yank in the R.A.F.* (1941), *Man Hunt* (1941) and *Sergeant York* (1941), which is actually a film about World War I.

Lady of Baseball." At the time Durocher was manager of the Chicago Cubs, my favorite team, she was no longer married to him.

George Sanders, Laraine Day, and Joel McCrea looking for spies in *Foreign Correspondent.*

2. *Sullivan's Travels* - 1941

Joel McCrea plays director John Sullivan who's tired of making silly comedies and musicals for his studio, like *Ants in Your Plants of 1939.* He wants to make films of social significance with a message about the troubles in today's world.

The problem is that he doesn't know anything about poverty and unemployment; for example, he's a rich kid who's been to boarding school. So off he sets, dressed like a tramp, to discover how the other half lives. ButSullivan's studio transforms his odyssey into a publicity stunt, providing the would-be hobo with a luxury van, complete with butler (Robert Greig) and valet (Eric Blore). Advised by his servants that the poor resent having the rich intrude upon them, Sullivan escapes his retinue and continues his travels incognito. En route, he meets a down-and-out failed actress (Veronica Lake). Experiencing firsthand the difficult existence of real-life hoboes, Sullivan returns to Hollywood full of bleeding-heart fervor.

After first arranging for the girl's screen test, he heads for the rail yards, intending to improve the lot of the local rail-riders by handing out ten thousand dollars in five-dollar bills. Instead, Sullivan is knocked out by a tramp, who steals Sullivan's clothes and identification. When the tramp is run over by a speeding train, the world at large is convinced that the great John L. Sullivan is dead. Meanwhile, the dazed Sullivan, dressed like a bum with no identification on his person, is arrested and put to work on a brutal Southern chain gang. With its almost Shakespearean combination of uproarious comedy and grim tragedy, *Sullivan's Travels* is director Preston Sturges' masterpiece and one of the finest movies about movies ever. Another good supporting cast includes William Demarest, Franklin Pangborn, Porter Hall, and Byron Foulger[91].

Veronica Lake said that this was one of her favorite films and she enjoyed working with Joel McCrea, in spite of their laughable height difference. [92]

Veronica Lake and Joel McCrea in *Sullivan's Travels*. They appear to be almost the same height in this shot.

3. *Ride the High Country* - 1962

---

91 Byron Foulger appeared in over 400 movies and television shows, which must be some kind of a record, including five directed by Preston Sturges. He was also Dr. Zarkov's assistant in the 1940 serial, *Flash Gordon Conquers the Universe*.

92 Veronica Lake was 4'11" while McCrea was almost 6'3".

Although *Ride the High Country* is technically outside the time period of this book, I had to include this classic Western film about two aging lawmen - Joel McCrea and Randolph Scott - in one last adventure together.

An aging ex-marshal Steve Judd (Joel McCrea) is hired by a bank to transport a gold shipment through dangerous territory. He hires an old partner, Gil Westrum (Randolph Scott, in a good role), and his young protégé Heck (Ron Starr) to assist him. Steve doesn't know, however, that Gil and Heck plan to steal the gold, with or without Steve's help. On the trail, the three get involved in a young woman (Mariette Hartley)'s desire to escape first from her father, then from her fiancé (James Drury in a rare role as a villain) and his dangerously psychotic brothers. A series of twists and turns takes place until the final shootout that pits Steve and Gil going it alone against the vile Hammond brothers.

Ride the Far Country might actually be Sam Peckinpah's best western. It examines the dying of the old West in the late 1800's or early 1900's in favor of a more modern West, without the gratuitous violence that we found in his later films, like *The Wild Bunch*. And Joel McCrea and Randolph Scott make an outstanding pairing - one always wanting to do the right thing while the other more interested in getting rich quick after years and years of being a low paid lawman.

An outstanding supporting cast also includes Edgar Buchanan as an immoral judge who gets his just desserts; R.G. Armstrong as a religious zealot father of Hartley; and L.Q. Jones, John Anderson, and Warren Oates as the other villainous Hammond brothers, who engage in the final shootout with McCrea and Scott.

Randolph Scott and Joel McCrea in one last ride together.

> This was the final film in the long career of Western star Randolph Scott. After seeing this film, he said he wanted to quit while he was ahead, believing that he could never do anything else as good as *Ride the High Country*.

4. *The More, the Merrier* - 1943

This 1943 World War II romantic comedy stars Joel McCrea and the wonderful Jean Arthur, with Charles Coburn also starring and winning an Oscar for his performance.

It's World War II and there is a severe housing shortage everywhere - especially in Washington, D.C. where the Federal bureaucracy has grown exponentially because of the war effort. Connie Milligan (Jean Arthur) rents an apartment and, believing it to be her patriotic duty, she offers to sublet half of her apartment, fully expecting a suitable female tenant. What she gets instead is mischievous, middle-aged Benjamin Dingle (Charles Coburn in probably the best role of his long career). Dingle talks her into subletting to him and then promptly sublets half of his half to young, irreverent Joe Carter (Joel McCrea) - creating a situation tailor-made for comedy and romance - hence, the title "The More, the Merrier."

The More, the Merrier is a funny yet moving film that reflects what life was like during the war. Joel McCrea and Jean Arthur are a perfect match, and McCrea demonstrates what a really good romantic comedy star he was. There is also a great scene in which a male factory worker has to run the gauntlet between a group of female workers at quitting time; he has to endure their hoots and catcalls from the Rosie the Riveters, which is a nice turn of events from what typically takes place in a workplace.

Charles Coburn made 99 films and had an almost 30-year career which did not even begin until he was almost 60.[93] Some of his best films

---

93   He was primarily a stage actor up until that time.

include *Monkey Business*, *The Lady Eve*, *Gentlemen Prefer Blondes*, and *King's Row*, where he played an unethical doctor who unnecessarily sawed off Ronald Reagan's legs after an accident, because he did not like him.

Character actor Charles Coburn

5. *The Palm Beach Story* - 1942

This film was another good early 1940s romantic comedy featuring Joel McCrea paired up with Claudette Colbert, another star from this book. Since this film was already listed in the section on Claudette Colbert, I will not repeat that information. But it is further evidence that Joel McCrea could do more than westerns.

6. *The Most Dangerous Game* - 1932

When I was in high school, we read a 1924 short story by Richard Connell called "The Most Dangerous Game" about a big-game hunter who falls off a yacht in the Caribbean. He swims to the shore where he is first welcomed and then hunted by a Russian aristocrat. At the time I thought that this story would make a really exciting movie. Little did I know that it had been made into a film some 30+ years previously.

The Most Dangerous Game is, in fact, an 1932 adventure film starring Joel McCrea, Fay Wray - a year before she made her most famous film, *King Kong*, and Leslie Banks. Closely following the short story, after the luxury cabin cruiser that he is a passenger on crashes on a reef, Bob Rainsford (Joel McCrea) finds himself washed ashore on a remote island. He comes upon a fortress-like house and the owner, Count Zaroff (Leslie Banks), seems to be quite welcoming. Apart from Zaroff's servant Ivan (Noble Johnson), the only other people present are Eve Trowbridge (Fay Wray) and her brother Martin (Robert Armstrong), also survivors of their own shipwreck. Other survivors are missing, however, and Rainsford soon learns why.

Zaroff releases them into his jungle island and then hunts them down in his grisly "outdoor chess" game! Then after Martin disappears, Bob realizes that he and Eve are to be the next "pawns" in Zaroff's deadly and most dangerous game. Zaroff makes what he considers a fair proposition: If Rainsford can stay alive until sunrise, Zaroff promises him and Eve their freedom. However, he has never lost the game of what he calls "outdoor chess."

In addition to Fay Wray, two other actors who appeared in this film also appeared in *King Kong*. Robert Armstrong had the lead role, as movie producer/director Carl Denham. and African-American actor Noble Johnson played the role of the native chief. *The Most Dangerous Game* is apparently the earliest known instance of a black actor working in white face to play a Caucasian, in this case a Russian named Ivan. And I have to believe that Joel McCrea would have made a much better leading man as John Driscoll than the rather wooden Bruce Cabot in *King Kong*..

Many of the sets from this film were also used in *King Kong*, which was made at roughly the same time as this film but was a much longer production and was released a year later.

African-American actor Noble Johnson as Ivan, the Russian servant, in *The Most Dangerous Game.*

7. *The Great Man's Lady* - 1942

A Joel McCrea/Barbara Stanwyck western (sort of) that covers a period of 80 years. In Hoyt City, a statue of founder Ethan Hoyt (Joel McCrea) is dedicated, and 100+ year old Hannah Sempler Hoyt - Barbara Stanwyck - (who lives in the last residence among skyscrapers), is at last persuaded to tell her story to a "girl biographer." Thus begins the flashback as Hannah tells her tale: In 1848, teenage Hannah meets and flirts with pioneer Ethan; on a sudden impulse, they elope. The film follows their struggles - and there are many of them - to found a city in the Western wilderness, hampered by the Gold Rush, star-crossed love, perils, and heartbreak.

While Joel McCrea is good in this film, the movie is really Barbara Stanwyck's. She ages over 80 years in the film, and is credible at any age. While not a great film, it represents a good early Joel McCrea western. A good supporting cast includes Brian Donlevy, K.T. Stevens as the biographer, and Thurston Hall.

> Barbara Stanwyck and Joel McCrea made a total of six films together. In addition to this film, they included *Union Pacific*, *Trooper Hook*, *Gambling Lady*, *Banjo on My Knee*, and *Internes Can't Make Money*. Stanwyck always considered Joel McCrea one of her favorite leading men.

While he was known mainly for Westerns, as I have attempted to portray, Joel McCrea was also a very good actor in romantic comedies and adventures/dramas. In fact, some of his best films were not westerns at all.

17. Cyd Charisse (1922-2008)

There were good female dancers, and then there was Cyd Charisse. Arguably the best female dancer of that period, she was also beautiful and glamorous, and a decent enough actress when she got a good role. Cyd Charisse was in perhaps the two best movie musicals of that era[94] - *The Bandwagon* and *Singin' in the Rain*. She was also the frequent dance partner of the two most famous male dancers in history - Gene Kelly and Fred Astaire. As Astaire once said about her, "When you've danced

---

94 As opposed to musicals that started out on Broadway, such as "Oklahoma,""Carousel,", "My Fair Lady," and "The Sound of Music."

with Cyd, you stay danced with." And in a sense, that was the legacy of the actress and dancer, whose sinuous style and breathtaking beauty captivated moviegoers during the 1940s and '50s. Charisse's on-screen visibility grew less frequent with the decline of the Hollywood musical in the late 1950s, though she could be glimpsed in occasional roles in films and on television for the next four decades before her death in 2008.

Biography

Born Tula Ellice Finklea in Amarillo, TX on March 8, 1922, her screen name came from a nickname given her by an older brother who could not pronounce "sis." Sickly from an early age after a bout with polio, she took dance lessons to regain her strength, and showed enough promise to warrant an audition with the Ballet Russes, which brought her talent to audiences both in the United States and in Europe. While in Europe, she was reunited with a young dancer she had trained with named Nico Charisse, and the couple got married in 1939 when she was 17. The outbreak of World War II sent her back to the United States, where she settled with her new husband in Los Angeles. While there, Ballet Russes star David Lichine tapped her to perform in a new feature, Gregory Ratoff's *Something to Shout About* (1943). The film was not a success, and though Charisse had no initial interest in becoming a movie actress, she was signed to a seven-year contract with MGM and joined the Freed Unit, which oversaw a pool of talent for MGM's musical films. She was soon put through the studio's rigorous grooming process, which included singing and elocution lessons to remove her Texas accent.

Charisse was unbilled for several of her early appearances; among these being *Ziegfeld Follies* (1944), in which she briefly shared the screen with one of her greatest future co-stars, Fred Astaire. Eventually, she worked her way up to featured dancer in a wide variety of musicals, which allowed her to show off her versatility in different styles of dance. Charisse also appeared in occasional dramatic roles in films like the noir *Tension* (1949) and *East Side, West Side* (1949), where her dark good looks were put to use as various femme fatales or ethnic types. As her career began to gain momentum, her marriage to Charisse came to an end in 1948, but she was soon married to popular crooner Tony

Martin, with whom she had a son, Tony Jr., in 1950.[95] Her pregnancy kept her from appearing opposite Gene Kelly in his landmark *An American in Paris* (1951), but the talented actor/choreographer/director remembered her for his next project.

That film, *Singin' in the Rain* (1952) became her breakout film. Cast after producer Freed sought a more skilled partner for Kelly in the film's climactic "Broadway Melody Ballet," she stunned audiences and critics alike with the depth and range of her talent, which were made all the more memorable by her dark loveliness. From her first appearance as a gangster's moll dressed in flapper green dress to the later romantic ballet, she impressed audiences with her beauty and talent. The film cemented her reputation as one of the most talented dancers in Hollywood, and she quickly followed its success with a starring role in another acclaimed film, *The Band Wagon* (1953), this time opposite Fred Astaire. Charisse played a ballerina who is chosen to perform opposite Astaire's fading movie star character.

Charisse was the co-star and dance partner of choice for Kelly and Astaire in some of their best efforts in the 1950s. She was Fiona Cooper, resident of *Brigadoon* (1954) and love interest to Kelly's bewildered traveler in Vincente Minnelli's film adaptation of the popular musical, and later co-starred with him in his final big-screen musical, *It's Always Fair Weather* (1955). She also appeared in Astaire's musical swan song, *Silk Stockings* (1957), a musical version of the Greta Garbo comedy *Ninotchka* with Charisse in the Garbo role. Her performance would earn her a Golden Globe nomination. When asked to name her favorite among the two screen dance legends, she cited that while Kelly was the more athletic dancer, both were "delicious" in their own way.[96]

The impact of television and rising production costs brought an end to the movie musical by the late fifties, but Charisse's acting ability allowed her to segue into straight dramatic roles for much of the next decade.

---

95 A marriage that lasted until her death in 2008.

96 Personally, while I always appreciated Astaire's ballroom excellence, I preferred Gene Kelly's athletic, blue-collar approach to dance even more.

For example, Nicholas Ray gave her a good part as a dancer in the cult favorite *Party Girl* (1958) with Robert Taylor.

By the mid-1960s, Charisse was making films mainly in Europe, where her poise and looks earned her regular employment in exotic, as well as regal roles. Television offered more opportunities for audiences to enjoy her abilities. She also performed in Las Vegas with husband Tony Martin as part of a successful nightclub act during these years. [97]

Charisse was an infrequent guest star in television dramas during the 1970s and '80s, and penned a tandem autobiography with Martin in 1976 titled *The Two of Us*. In the 1990s she appeared in several music videos and also followed in the footsteps of her former co-star Debbie Reynolds by releasing her own senior-oriented exercise video, "Easy Energy Shape Up," in 1990.

In 2006 Cyd Charisse was given the National Medal of the Arts and Humanities by President George W. Bush in a private ceremony at the White House. On June 16 2008, Charisse was admitted to Cedars-Sinai Hospital after suffering from a reported heart attack; she died the following day at the age of 86, one of the last surviving of the MGM musical stars during that genre's heyday.

Awards

Cyd Charisse was nominated for a Golden Globe and a Laurel Award for her performance in *Silk Stockings* in 1958.

My favorite Cyd Charisse Films

Of course, five out of six are musicals but I also threw in one drama that was pretty good.

1. *The Band Wagon* - 1953
2. *Singin' in the Rain* - 1952
3. *Brigadoon* - 1954
4. *It's Always Fair Weather* - 1955
5. *Party Girl* - 1958
6. *Silk Stockings* - 1957

---

97   I actually saw their act in Las Vegas in the 60s.

1. *The Band Wagon* - 1953

The Band Wagon isa lavish, enduring backstage 1953 musical from Vincente Minnelli. *The Band Wagon* tells the story of Tony Hunter (Fred Astaire, who was 54 at the time) a multi-talented but aging movie star who heads for the Great White Way in hopes of bolstering his declining career. His two talented pals in New York, Lily and Les Martin (Nanette Fabray and Oscar Levant, who are both excellent in their roles), are only too happy to help out by writing him a dazzling play. Unfortunately, for a lot of reasons, including the fact that there is great tension between Tony and his leggy co-star Gabrielle Gerard (Cyd Charisse) because she thinks him too old and he thinks her too tall, the production bombs. Plus, the fact that the play is extremely pretentious and poorly directed by Jeffrey Cordova (Jack Buchanan) does not help at all.

Fortunately this failure only inspires the cast and crew to work even harder until they eventually rewrite the entire musical, which ends up succeeding beyond their wildest dreams. Some of the most memorable songs include: "Dancing in the Dark (beautifully danced by Astaire and Charisse),""Triplets," and "That's Entertainment." In "Triplets," Nanette Fabray, Fred Astaire, and Jack Buchanan play toddlers who dance on their knees (or at least appear to do so.) And "That's Entertainment" is pretty much the showstopper of showstoppers when it comes to musicals.

Cyd Charisse's acting is decent enough, but it is her dance numbers with Fred Astaire that are truly spectacular. The movie was nominated for Oscars for Best Writing, Best Costume Design, and Best Musical Score.[98]*The Band Wagon*, along with *Singin' in the Rain*, are clearly the crown jewels of the original movie musical of the 1950s.

Everything about the film is spectacular, and it remains fresh to this day. If you have not seen it, it is a must view.

---

98 It lost out on Best Musical Score to *Call Me Madam*, which was definitely a poor choice on the part of Academy voters, in my opinion.

Cyd Charisse and Fred Astaire in the spectacular "Dancing in the Dark" number from _The Bandwagon_. Two of the best dancers ever in a spectacular approach to this song.

2. *Singin' in the Rain* - 1952

We follow *The Bandwagon* with perhaps the greatest movie musical ever made by Hollywood - *Singin' in the Rain*. The major difference from the perspective of this book is that Cyd Charisse is not the female lead in this film, but only appears in one long scene, the wonderful "Broadway Melody Ballet" number that she dances with Gene Kelly near the end of the film.

Basically, the plot of the film is the change in Hollywood moving from silent films to "talkies" and the effect on the studios and some of the stars. Some stars moved from silent films to talkies without any problems, while some as in this case Lina Lamont (in a brilliant performance by Jean Hagen) had a huge problem because of her New York accent that was really annoying.

In 1927 Hollywood, Monumental Pictures' biggest stars, glamorous on-screen couple Lina Lamont (Jean Hagen) and Don Lockwood (Gene Kelly), are also an off-screen couple if the trade papers and gossip columns are to be believed. Both perpetuate the public perception if only to please their adoring fans, bring people into the movie theaters, and stay employed. In reality, Don barely tolerates her, while Lina, despite thinking Don beneath her, simplemindedly believes what she sees on screen in order to bolster her own stardom and sense of self-importance. R.F. Simpson, Monumental's head, (Millard Mitchell) dismisses what he thinks is a flash in the pan: talking pictures.

It isn't until *The Jazz Singer* (1927) becomes a bona fide hit which results in all the movie theaters installing sound equipment that R.F. knows Monumental, most specifically in the form of Don and Lina, needs to jump on the talking picture bandwagon, despite no one at the studio knowing anything about the technology, including where to place the microphones. Musician Cosmo Brown (Donald O'Connor), Don's best friend, gets hired as Monumental's musical director. While this is going on, Don becomes enamored with Kathy Selden (Debbie Reynolds), a local singer/dancer, who he literally meets by dropping in on her from above while she is driving.

Cosmo comes up with the brilliant idea of turning their latest production into a musical and renaming it "The Dancing Cavalier." Unfortunately, not only can't Lina sing or dance, she really can't act and has that extremely annoying New York accent. So they get Kathy Selden to agree to dub in her lines and sing for her. Within "The Dancing Cavalier" is a scene featuring the Broadway Melody Ballet which is spectacularly danced by Gene Kelly and Cyd Charisse.

If you ever wanted to pick a single dance number which says it all about musicals, you could probably pick this number. Kelly and Charisse are wonderful together, and the scene is at the same time very beautiful and very erotic. Cyd Charisse is gorgeous, and the two of them dance as one.[99]

While all of the musical numbers are terrific, the two other ones that stand out are Gene Kelly singing the title song in a pouring rain and Donald O'Connor's rendition of "Make 'em Laugh." I don't think I have ever seen a dance more acrobatic than O'Connor's in "Make 'em Laugh." As they say - often imitated but never equaled.

---

99 To make things even more perfect, both of them were 5'8" tall.

If *The Band Wagon* is a great American movie musical, *Singin' in the Rain* is even one notch higher. Voted by the American Film Institute as the 10th best American movie of all time, it is a well-deserved ranking. Surprisingly, the film was nominated for only two Oscars, Best Musical Score and Best Supporting Actress (Hagen) and did not win either. Donald O'Connor did win a Best Actor - Comedy or Musical Golden Globe, and the film was nominated as Best Picture - Comedy or Musical but lost out to *With a Song in My Heart*, a good movie but nowhere in the class of *Singin' in the Rain*. And it holds up, after 65 years.

Gene Kelly and Cyd Charisse in the spectacular Broadway Melody Ballet scene.

Millard Mitchell was an interesting character actor. While he played the studio head in this film, he also played in lots of good westerns, including *The Gunfighter* with Gregory Peck, *The Naked Spur* with James Stewart, and was Stewart's pal in *Winchester '73*. A heavy smoker, Mitchell unfortunately died of lung cancer at the age of 50.

3. *Brigadoon* - 1954

In this movie version of the hit Broadway musical, Cyd Charisse is once again the female lead opposite her (probable) favorite dancing partner, Gene Kelly.

American businessmen from New York City Tommy Albright (Gene Kelly) and Jeff Douglas (Van Johnson, in a good supporting role as his comic relief pal), are on a hunting vacation in Scotland. While they are lost, they discover a quaint and beautiful village, Brigadoon. Strangely, the village is not on any map, and soon Tommy and Jeff find out why: Brigadoon is an enchanted place that seems to be from the 1800s. They learn from the local scribe that, because of a desire by the minister to protect the village and ward off evil outside influences, Brigadoon appears once every hundred years for one day, then disappears back into the mists of time, to wake up to its next day a century later. When Tommy falls in love with Fiona (Cyd Charisse), a girl of the village, he realizes that she can never be part of his life back in America. But can he be part of hers in Brigadoon?

So tell me, would you rather be part of the New York City rat race, or spend the rest of your days with Cyd Charisse? To me, the answer is easy, but when Tommy returns to New York, he realizes what a mistake he made by not staying. But can he get a second chance?

Lots of great singing and dancing, especially by Gene Kelly and Cyd Charisse, and Van Johnson is really not a bad dancer at all. His scenes with a local girl (Dodie Heath) trying to seduce him into marriage are very funny. And several of the numbers are really good, my favorites being "Go Home with Bonnie Jean,""Heather on the Hill," and "Almost Like Being in Love," one of the all-time great musical numbers. Kelly does more ballet dancing than tap dancing in this film, and "Go Home with Bonnie Jean" brings the entire male cast together in a rousing production number. Cyd Charisse is beautiful, her dancing is wonderful, and her acting is just fine for this production.

About the only criticism is that the scenes in Brigadoon look a bit stagy, like they were filmed on a Hollywood set (which they were) instead of in a more natural setting.

Brigadoon was nominated for three Academy Awards - best art/set decoration, best costume design, and best sound, but won none. However, it did win a Golden Globe for Best Cinematography.

All in all, Brigadoon is one of my five favorite musicals so I loved the movie version of this Broadway hit.

I loved watching **Gene Kelly** and **Cyd Charisse** dance in *Brigadoon.*

4. *It's Always Fair Weather* - 1955

Another good musical from 1955 with Gene Kelly and Cyd Charisse which doesn't get as much of a following today, but is still a good film. And Cyd Charisse gets to do more acting in this one and is very good!

Ted, Doug, and Angie (Gene Kelly, Dan Dailey, and Michael Kidd[100]) are three ex-G.I.s from World War II who vow to meet again at their

---

100 Michael Kidd was one of the best choreographers around. *Seven Brides for Seven Brothers* and *The Bandwagon* are among his credits.

favorite New York City bar on October 11, 1955, ten years to the day after they got out of the service. They all show up on the appointed day, but quickly find that their friendship isn't what it used to be. Not only is that the case, but they really can't stand one another.

However, an advertising executive - Jackie Leighton (Cyd Charisse) hears about their story and decides that it would be a great idea to bring the three men together again on a live TV show. She and Ted meet at a local gym, where Jackie demonstrates her knowledge of boxing in front of a group of beefy boxers, in a dance called "Baby, You Knock Me Out."

Circumstances are further complicated by a group of gangsters who are after Ted, a boxing promoter who has refused to fix a fight. The gangsters follow him to the television program, where Doug and Angie come to Ted's aid, and the three of them dispose of the gangsters. After that, they become friends again but part without any plans for getting together again.

While the movie received excellent reviews, MGM did not promote it that much, instead placing it in a double bill with the Western classic *Bad Day at Black Rock*. Perhaps it was the somewhat depressing theme (you can't go home again, basically). In any case, the principals were wonderful, with Kelly, Dailey, and Charisse particularly good in their dance numbers. And Dan Dailey holds his own in his dance scenes with two great dancers - Gene Kelly and Michael Kidd.

It's Always Fair Weather received two Oscar nominations - for Betty Comden and Apolph Green for Best Screenplay and Andre Previn for Best Scoring of a musical, but did not win either award. The supporting cast included Dolores Gray and Jay C. Flippen.

Michael Kidd, Gene Kelly, and Dan Dailey dancing on trash can lids in *It's Always Fair Weather*.

> Betty Comden and Adolph Green collaborated together for almost 60 years and won seven Tony awards. Among their works were "On the Town,""Singin' in the Rain,""Bells Are Ringing," and "Applause." They worked together for so long that most people assumed they were married, which was not the case.

5. *The Party Girl* - 1958

I decided to throw in a drama with Cyd Charisse in a good role, and chose 1958's *The Party Girl*, which paired Cyd with Robert Taylor.

Lawyer Thomas Farrell (Robert Taylor) has made a career defending crooks in trials, primarily for mob boss Rico Angelo (Lee J. Cobb). He's not particularly happy about it, but it has made him a successful and wealthy man. His most recent triumph is defending Louis Canetto (John Ireland) on a murder charge. Farrell has never realized that there is a downside to his success, until he meets the dancer Vicki Gaye (Cyd Charisse). She makes him decide to get a better reputation by getting out of this seamy business. But mob king Rico Angelo insists that he continue his services. So for the first time in his working life, he has to make some tough decisions.

Cyd Charisse is good in a dramatic role, but Robert Taylor is a big surprise, as he is extremely believable as the lawyer who wants to change his life for the better. As usual, Lee J. Cobb is over the top as the mob boss, but a really scary guy. Cyd Charisse does a couple of dance numbers, but it really is not a musical, and the dance numbers almost seem misplaced in a good drama. And the title "Party Girl" is really a misnomer - she's a dancer who is not really a party girl.

Overall, a good film and sort of a color film noir. This marked the final film for Robert Taylor under his MGM contract; he held the record for the longest career as an MGM contract player. And Director Nicholas Ray was really impressed with Taylor's dedication to be believable in his role.

6. *Silk Stockings* - 1957

Silk Stockings is essentially A musical remake of *Ninotchka*: After three bumbling Soviet agents fail in their mission to retrieve a straying Soviet composer from Paris, the beautiful, ultra-serious Ninotchka (Cyd Charisse) is sent to complete their mission and to retrieve them. She starts out condemning the decadent West, but gradually falls under its spell, with the help of Steve Canfield (Fred Astaire), an American movie producer.

After this film, Fred Astaire effectively retired from musicals, preferring to concentrate on non-musical roles, though he would produce several musical specials for TV in the next few years. Astaire wouldn't make another musical until 1968.

Many people consider the film version of *Silk Stockings* to be a decided improvement on the stage version because of the emphasis on dance, as nothing else could have so movingly and convincingly conveyed Ninotchka's transformation from Communist to Capitalist. Indeed, Charisse's solo interpretation of the title song, which charts the character's carefully preconceived -- and humorously concealed -- shift in allegiance, did not exist on stage, and emerged as the centerpiece of the film.

Cyd Charisse's vocals were dubbed in by Carole Richards, who also sung for her in *Brigadoon* and *It's Always Fair Weather*. But Cyd did her own dancing, of course! And a good supporting cast includes Peter Lorre, Jules Munshin, and Joseph Buloff as the three Russian spies, George Tobias as her Russian boss, and Janis Paige.

> The musical numbers were composed by Cole Porter, one of my favorite American composers. This was, frankly, not one of his better efforts, although "All of You" is an excellent song. But it pales in comparison to *Kiss Me Kate*, for example.

Everything considered, Cyd Charisse was one of the best female dancers in musicals and ranks right up there with her male counterparts, Gene Kelly and Fred Astaire. She brought a sensuality to the dance that many of the other female dancers did not possess. While not a great actress, she was competent enough to be effective in musicals and other roles.

18. Edward G. Robinson (1893-1973)

The more I see of Edward G. Robinson, the more I like him. Very likely less famous than Cagney or Bogart, that probably makes him ideal for a book on forgotten movie stars.

We always think of him as playing gangsters, but he was much more than that. Later in his career, "Eddie" played a much larger variety of roles. In real life, he had a much softer side, was an art collector, and was always viewed as a good guy to work with. Edward G. Robinson had an extremely long and illustrious career in films, from a cameo role in 1916's *Arms and the Woman* as a factory worker all the way to his last role in the 1973 film *Soylent Green*. And he was always much, much more than just Little Caesar.

Biography

Edward G. Robinson, whose original name was Emanuel Goldenberg, was born Dec. 12, 1893 in Bucharest, Romania and died Jan. 26, 1973 in Hollywood, California. He was an American stage and of course film actor who skillfully played a wide range of character types but who is best known for his portrayals of gangsters and criminals.

Although he was born in Romania, he emigrated with his parents at age ten and grew up on New York's Lower East Side. He gave up early dreams of becoming either a rabbi or a lawyer and while a student at City College settled on acting. After winning a scholarship in 1911 to the American Academy of Dramatic Arts, Robinson made his stage debut in "Paid in Full"in 1913. His knowledge of many languages helped him win a multilingual part in "Under Fire in 1915," his Broadway debut. He continued acting each Broadway season for the next decade, and in 1927 he had his first starring role, in the play "The Racket."

Though he had appeared in two silent films—*Arms and the Woman* (1916) and *The Bright Shawl* (1923)—it was not until the advent of sound that Robinson's movie career began in earnest. After a few undistinguished dramas, he starred as the trigger-happy gangster Enrico Bandello in *Little Caesar*(1931). It was the perfect part for Edward G. Robinson and made him an instant movie star. Robinson's dynamic performance, like that of James Cagney in *The Public Enemy* (1931), made the film stand apart from the usual underworld story, and both films marked the start of a long series of gangster pictures with which the Warner Brothers studio would become most associated throughout the 1930s and '40s. Most of them seemed to star Robinson, Cagney, or Humphrey Bogart, or a combination of the three.

Short, chubby, with "the face of a depraved cherub and a voice which makes everything he says seem violently profane," as *Time* magazine described him in 1931, Robinson was content that his career would consist of rough-and-tumble roles and character parts; he was happy to turn what would have otherwise been physical drawbacks into instantly identifiable trademarks. He continued playing "tough mugs" in film after film: a con man in *Smart Money* (1931), a cigar-chomping newspaper editor in *Five Star Final* (1931), a convicted murderer in *Two Seconds* (1932), and a spoof of his own Little Caesar image in *The Little Giant* (1933). *The Whole Town's Talking* (1935), in which he played the dual roles of a timid bank clerk and a ruthless hoodlum, showed

Robinson capable of fine, understated comedy, whereas in *Bullets or Ballots* (1936), he at last got to play somebody on the right side of the law, an undercover policeman. And in 1937 he began a five-year run on the popular radio series *Big Town*, playing a newspaper editor.

Robinson considered his title role in *Dr. Ehrlich's Magic Bullet* (1940) to be his best performance. The story of the doctor who found the cure for syphilis, the film was further proof that Robinson could give a distinguished performance even without a gun in his hand or a cigar in his mouth. His other well-received films include *A Dispatch from Reuters* (1940), *The Sea Wolf* (1941), *Double Indemnity* (1944), *The Woman in the Window* (1944), *Our Vines Have Tender Grapes* (1945), *All My Sons* (1948), and *Key Largo* (1948).

In the 1950s Robinson suffered a series of personal setbacks. He testified several times for the House Committee on Un-American Activities before he was ultimately cleared of any wrongdoing, and a divorce settlement in 1956 forced him to sell off most of his private art collection, which was considered one of the finest in the world. Still, he kept working in films and returned to Broadway in Paddy Chayefsky's "Middle of the Night" (1956). By the 1950s he was no longer a major star, though he continued to deliver fine performances in notable films such as *The Ten Commandments* (1956),[101] *A Hole in the Head* (1959), and *The Cincinnati Kid* (1965). Eddie also had a number of good roles on television and guest-starred in many dramas and specials, including *Ford Theatre*, *Playhouse 90*, and Rod Serling's *Night Gallery*.

Robinson died in 1973 shortly after completing his final film, *Soylent Green*. He was married twice and had one son, Edward G. Robinson, Jr. Robinson was posthumously awarded a special Oscar for his contributions to the art of motion pictures.

Awards

---

101 The typical Cecil B. DeMille film with great special effects like the parting of the Red Sea and dopey dialogue, although Robinson's performance was very good.

It is hard to believe, but Edward G. Robinson was never nominated for an Oscar. However, as I indicated, he did receive an honorary Oscar in 1973 for greatness as a performer, a patron of the arts, and a dedicated citizen.

Robinson won a Best Actor award at the Cannes Film Festival in 1949 for his performance in *House of Strangers*. He was nominated for a Laurel Award in 1966 for his performance in *The Cincinnati Kid* with Steve McQueen. And he received a Lifetime Achievement Award from the Screen Actors Guild in 1970.

My favorite Edward G. Robinson films

I have tried to choose from among a group of film genres, not just crime films. Again, these are MY favorite films of his, not necessarily THE BEST (although some are his best).

1. *Double Indemnity* - 1944
2. *Little Caesar* - 1931
3. *Key Largo* - 1948
4. *Brother Orchid* - 1940
5. *Scarlet Street* - 1945
6. *The Stranger* - 1946
7. *The Sea Wolf* - 1941

1. *Double Indemnity* - 1944

Yes, Barbara Stanwyck and Fred MacMurray are the two leads. Barbara Stanwcyk was nominated for an Oscar and should have won, and Fred MacMurray's performance is not like any other role you have seen him in, certainly not Steve Douglas on the *My Three Sons* television show. But it is Edward G. Robinson's performance that holds the film together and one of the reasons why this is my single favorite performance of his.

Walter Neff (Fred MacMurray) is an insurance salesman who makes a routine stop at the house of one of his customers to remind him that his auto insurance policy is up for renewal. The client is not home but his seductive wife, Phyllis Dietrichson (Barbara Stanwyck) certainly is.

She asks about taking out an insurance policy on her husband without him knowing. At first, he does not want any part of this scheme, but when she shows up at his apartment and proposes that they murder him, he is hooked. And of course, as an insurance specialist, he proposes that they make her husband's death look like an accident so that they can collect a "double indemnity" on his death due to an accident. Her husband is supposed to take the train to attend an old college reunion, which is the perfect setting for the murder. After they murder her husband in the car, and throw his body on the train tracks, implying that he fell off the train, Phyllis applies to collect the money through Walter's company.

That is where Edward G. Robinson (Barton Keyes) takes over. As the insurance analyst and Walter's best friend, the "little man" inside him tells him there is something wrong here. He does not believe it was an accident and doesn't think he committed suicide either; he thinks Mr. Dietrichson was murdered. In fact, he thinks Phyllis murdered him with the help of another man. That is when things start to unravel for Walter and Phyllis. Instead of double indemnity, what we get is double cross, with both of the principals trying to do in the other one.

Robinson is simply brilliant as the crusty, persistent, and single-minded insurance reviewer. At one point he tells Walter and the CEO, Mr. Norton, why he thinks it could not possibly be suicide with the following explanation:

"You know, you, uh, ought to take a look at the statistics on suicide sometime. You might learn a little something about the insurance business...Come now, you've never read an actuarial table in your life, have you? Why, they've got 10 volumes on suicide alone. Suicide by race, by color, by occupation, by sex, by seasons of the year, by time of day. Suicide, how committed: by poisons, by firearms, by drowning, by leaps. Suicide by poison, subdivided by types of poison, such as corrosive, irritant, systemic, gaseous, narcotic, alkaloid, protein, and so forth. Suicide by leaps, subdivided by leaps from high places, under the wheels of trains, under the wheels of trucks, under the feet of horses, from steamboats. But Mr. Norton, of all the cases on record, there's not one single case of suicide by leap from the rear end of a moving train." I bet you don't talk to your CEO like that!

He won't give up, and that ends up in getting Walter and Phyllis the result they deserved.

Double Indemnity was nominated for seven Academy Awards, including Best Picture, Best Director (Billy Wilder), and Best Actress (Stanwyck) but unbelievably did not win any. It is probably the single best example of film noir[102] of any movie, and it is simply a must see. The International Movie Data Base rates it as one of the best 100 American movies ever made. While there is a good supporting cast, these three individuals really are the whole film.

Fred MacMurray discussing insurance with Barbara Stanwyck but definitely has more than insurance on his mind in *Double Indemnity*.

2. *Little Caesar* - 1931

---

102 Again, film noir is a cinematic term used primarily to describe stylish Hollywood crime dramas, particularly those that emphasize cynical attitudes and sexual motivations. Hollywood's classical film noir period is generally regarded as extending from the early 1940s to the late 1950s. These films are generally in black and white rather than color and often feature a conniving femme fatale.

This was Edward G. Robinson's real first starring role, and the film that catapulted his career after that. It was released the same year Warner Brothers also released *Public Enemy*, which made a star of James Cagney.

Enrico Bandello (Edward G. Robinson) is a small-time hood who knocks off gas stations for whatever he can take - not exactly a mob boss. But he heads east to Chicago along with his friend Joe Massara (Douglas Fairbanks, Jr.) and signs up with Sam Vettori's mob. While there, Joe decides he wants nothing to do with a life of crime and instead becomes a dancer and meets a new dance partner and girl friend, Olga (Glenda Farrell). But Rico forces him, at least temporarily, to work as the gang's lookout man until Joe sees some people gunned down by Rico.

A New Year's Eve robbery at Little Arnie Lorch's casino results in the death of the crime commissioner Alvin McClure. Rico is ambitious and eventually takes over Vettori's gang; he then moves up to the next echelon pushing out Diamond Pete Montana. When he orders Joe to dump his girlfriend Olga and re-join the gang, Olga decides there's only one way out for them, so she calls Police Sergeant Flaherty and provides information on the gang. With that, Flaherty proceeds to crush the gang. As he is dying from a gunshot wound, Rico utters the famous line: "Mother of Mercy, is this the end of Rico?"

The opening week of *Little* Caesar's release broke the all-time attendance record for Warner Bros. Strand Theatre in New York, grossing $50,000. Edward G. Robinson and Douglas Fairbanks Jr. made personal appearances at the New York premiere, for which the top ticket price was $2.00, quite a sum for a movie ticket in 1931, especially during the Great Depression.

Little Caesar was also one of the first big parts for actor Douglas Fairbanks, Jr., the son of silent film legend Douglas Fairbanks. Fairbanks, Jr. went on to play a number of swashbuckling parts, including *The Prisoner of Zenda* and *Sinbad, the Sailor*. He was an extremely handsome actor but also very bright: Fairbanks was successful in business and politics as well.

Douglas Fairbanks, Jr. in one of his famous swashbuckling roles. He was of course the son of Douglas Fairbanks, one of the biggest stars of silent films.

3. *Key Largo* - 1947

Key Largo is a 1947 film noir/drama that features two of the big three stars from the gangster films of the 1930s - Humphrey Bogart and Edward G. Robinson. This time, Bogart is the hero, while Robinson is the villain.

Frank McCloud (Humphrey Bogart) travels to a run-down hotel on Key Largo, Florida to honor the memory of a friend who died bravely in his unit during WW II. His friend's widow, Nora Temple (Lauren Bacall), and wheelchair-bound father, James Temple (Lionel Barrymore) manage the hotel and receive him warmly, but the three of them soon find themselves virtual prisoners when the hotel is taken over by a mob of gangsters led by Johnny Rocco (Edward G. Robinson), who hole up there to await the passing of a hurricane. Mr. Temple strongly detests Rocco but due to his infirmities can only confront him verbally. Having become disillusioned by the violence of war, Frank is reluctant to act, but Rocco's demeaning treatment of his alcoholic girl friend, Gaye Dawn (Claire Trevor) disgusts him. Rocco's involvement in the deaths of some innocent Seminole Indians and a deputy sheriff then start to motivate McCloud to overcome his inaction.

Bogart is good, but the real star of the film is clearly Robinson. He is the essence of the slimy gangster with absolutely no redeeming values, and he drives the film forward after the hurricane passes. He forces his girl friend to sing a song a cappella, then berates her performance as well as her fading looks. And Claire Trevor won a Best Supporting Actress Oscar for her performance as the girlfriend.

Interestingly, although they played on-screen enemies, off-screen Humphrey Bogart and Robinson treated each other with great respect. Bogart insisted Robinson be treated like a major star and would not come to the set until the latter was ready. Often, he would go to Robinson's trailer to personally escort him to the set.

Key Largo is a truly outstanding movie, directed by the great John Huston. The plot is outstanding, and the dialog is even better. This is a film not to be missed.

4. *Brother Orchid* - 1940

I chose this film because it is a complete switch from the gangster persona often played by Edward G. Robinson.[103] This time Robinson is the good guy - more or less - while Humphrey Bogart is the heel.

Gang boss Little John Sarto (Edward G. Robinson) returns from Europe where he was looking for "class," to find the new gang leader Jack Buck (Humphrey Bogart) unwilling to relinquish his control. When Sarto puts together a rival gang, he gets wounded and seeks refuge in a monastery. He is gradually transformed by the simple, sincere brothers and, after one last gangland appearance, decides he has found class at last in the monastery overseen by Brother Superior (Donald Crisp). Of course, it's the monastery of the "Little Brothers of the Flower." (Hence the title of the film.) His unique talents prove very useful to the monks...especially when Sarto's old mob forces them out of the flower business.

Little John sees to it that Buck is brought to justice, and also fixes up his true-blue girlfriend, Flo Addams (Ann Sothern), with good-hearted

---

103 Although he does start out as a gangster in this one.

Texas rancher Clarence Fletcher (Ralph Bellamy). Sarto, now known as "Brother Orchid," returns to the monastery for good, declaring that he's finally found the real class that he always sought.

Not a great film, but a very good one, with Robinson moving from gangster to good guy monk. Interestingly, of the five films that Robinson and Bogart made together, this is the only one in which neither guy was killed. Other co-stars include Allen Jenkins, Cecil Kellaway, and John Ridgely.

5. *Scarlett Street* - 1945

I picked this one because Edward G. Robinson plays a nebbish who gets completely outfoxed by a woman and her boyfriend. Quite an unusual role for him.

At a dinner celebrating twenty-five years of employment, cashier Christopher Cross (Edward G. Robinson) is awarded an engraved watch by his boss, J. J. Hogarth, who later leaves the party with a stunning blonde, which impresses Chris. Walking home, Chris breaks up a violent quarrel between a man and a woman and, after the man flees, offers to escort the woman home. She introduces herself as Katherine "Kitty" March (Joan Bennett in a very effective role) and asks Chris to buy her a drink. Flattered and hoping to impress Kitty, Chris tells her that he is an artist and his modesty prompts her to suspect he is wealthy. The next day, Chris, who has been relegated by his shrewish wife Adele to practice his painting in the bathroom, grows depressed when she berates him for his lack of talent, and points out that her first husband died bravely as a detective.

Frustrated, Chris continues to see Kitty after that. Kitty's conniving boyfriend Johnny (Dan Duryea, in another good role as a scumbag), the man who beat her, also believes Chris is rich and pressures Kitty to date him. At home, as Adele's nagging continues, Chris steals some of the security bonds left by her deceased first husband. Johnny helps Kitty select a lavish studio and demands she ask Chris for more. When that is not enough, Chris begins stealing money from work, just to keep Kitty.

Johnny, certain Chris is a famous artist, takes some of his paintings to a street vendor, who assesses them as amateurish, but offers to try and sell them as Kitty's work. An art critic is impressed enough to offer to place the paintings with a prominent art dealer. When Chris finds out about this, he is at first upset but then pleased the paintings are selling and relieved to continue working in anonymity.

When Chris tells Kitty of his love for her, Kitty ridicules Chris and admits she has always loved Johnny. Outraged, Chris stabs Kitty to death with an ice pick and slips away as Johnny comes back to the studio. The next day at work, an audit of the books reveals Chris's embezzlement, and Chris is fired. Johnny is arrested and tried for Kitty's murder, then is executed, while Chris remains silent.

Guilt-ridden over the deaths of Kitty and Johnny, Chris attempts to hang himself, but is saved by neighbors. The haunted Chris takes to wandering the streets, trying to convince the police of his guilt, while the art gallery sells the "self portrait" of Kitty for an enormous fee. How ironic!

While the public did not like this movie[104], thinking it was too depressing, it is in many cases a masterpiece. Directed by Fritz Lang, who had a habit of directing rather bizarre films or crime films (see *M* and *While the City Sleeps*[105] as examples), it is a tense crime drama with some very creative plots and subplots. And the three leads are all outstanding.

---

104 In fact, censor boards in several major cities called the film "licentious, profane, obscure, and contrary to the good order of the community."

105 A good crime drama about a serial killer in New York City from the point of view of a large newspaper, starring Dana Andrews, Rhonda Fleming, Vincent Price, George Sanders, Ida Lupino, and Thomas Mitchell. What a cast!

Dan Duryea almost always played villains, especially really slimy, mean ones. But in real life he was one of the nicest people you would ever meet. Long married (35 years) to Helen Bryan until she died in 1967 and a family man at heart (he was once a scoutmaster and PTA parent!), he had two children. I guess that's why they call it acting.

6. *The Stranger* - 1946

Another good Edward G. Robinson film. This time he is an investigator from the War Crimes Commission who travels to a small New England town in search of a former Nazi war criminal.

A mild-mannered man identified only as Mr. Wilson of the War Crimes Commission (Edward G. Robinson) is seeking Franz Kindler (who turns out to be Orson Welles), mastermind of the Holocaust who came up with the idea of death camps and massive annihilation, and who has effectively erased his identity after the war. Wilson releases Kindler's former comrade Meinike and follows him to Harper, Connecticut, where he arrives on Kindler's wedding day and is killed by Kindler before he can identify him. Now Wilson's only clue is Kindler's fascination with antique clocks; but, though Kindler seems secure in his new identity, with a new fiancé (Loretta Young), he feels his past closing in. To make things even worse, Kindler is hiding out at an all-boys school as a professor named Charles Rankin.

Made in black and white and with a dark tint, the film has an eerie feeling throughout that is perfect for this plot. At first, we as the viewer think that perhaps Wilson is on a witch hunt and obviously has the wrong man, but as the film moves forward, we start to think differently.

Made in 1946, *The Stranger* is the first mainstream American film to show footage of Nazi concentration camps. Although Orson Welles apparently did not like the film, it is the only movie directed by Welles to show a profit in its original release. Suffice it to say that clocks and a clock tower play a significant role in this film.

Overall, I enjoyed the film very much. It was nice to see Edward G. Robinson playing the good guy for a change. *The Stranger* was nominated for a Best Writing Oscar but did not win.

Orson Welles and Edward G. Robinson in *The Stranger*. By this point in the film, we know the villain from the hero.

7. *The Sea Wolf* - 1941

In this 1941 film, Edward G. Robinson played a villain on the high seas. Based on the novel by Jack London, *The Sea Wolf* tells the story of three drifters who are "rescued" by a ship, "Ghost," and its cruel captain, Wolf Larsen.

Humphrey van Weyden (Alexander Knox), a writer, and escaped convict Ruth Webster (Ida Lupino) are aboard a ferry boat that collides with another ship and sinks. They are rescued and given refuge aboard the seal-hunting ship "Ghost," captained by the cruel Wolf Larsen. Also aboard as a reluctant crew member is George Leach (John Garfield). When Leach becomes too rebellious for his own good, Larsen replaces him as cabin boy with van Weyden. The crew mutinies against Larsen's brutal measures, but Larsen foils their mutiny and regains control of the ship.

Eventually van Weyden, Ruth, and George try to escape Larsen's clutches in a small dory, but find he has replaced their water with vinegar, so they reluctantly return to the ship. After a series of adventures when they return, things are eventually resolved, and not in Wolf Larsen's favor.

The Sea Wolf is a stirring adventure story with a good plot and cast, including Barry Fitzgerald, Howard Da Silva, and Gene Lockhart. Garfield is heroic in a tough guy role, and Robinson's Wolf Larsen is a complex character - he is well read and educated, but does not appreciate the value of education; plus, he is mean and nasty toward everyone, even Ruth Webster.

The Sea Wolf is directed by one of the great Hollywood directors of all time, Michael Curtiz. He gave us great films such as:
1. *Casablanca*
2. *The Adventures of Robin Hood*
3. *White Christmas*
4. *Captain Blood*
5. *Mildred Pierce*, and
6. *Yankee Doodle Dandy*

The Sea Wolf was nominated for one Oscar, Best Special Effects, but did not win.

211

I need to say a word or two about Ida Lupino. In addition to being a movie star herself, with over 100 film and television credits, she was also one of Hollywood's first female directors, with several films and many television credits. She was also married to one of my favorites, Louis Hayward, and later on to actor Howard Duff. Lupino was only the second female to be admitted into the Director's Guild.

Ida Lupino, a real trailblazer for women in films. She was as tough as Bette Davis, so they say.

As you can see, Edward G Robinson was an outstanding actor in virtually every film he was in - whether he was the villain or the hero. A man of profound artistic interests, he was acting up until the very end.

He co-starred with Charlton Heston in *Soylent Green*, which was finished ten days before his death. Robinson was an unforgettable movie star!

19. Gloria Grahame (1923-1981)

Gloria Grahame was a very alluring, captivating movie star who was also a good actress. She won one Oscar and was nominated for another. Her best work took place in the late 1940s and early 1950s, when she was in her early to late 30s. Unfortunately, her private life was rather tempestuous, including marital problems and child custody battles. Of her 64 film and television credits, Grahame was especially good in film noir movies, with at least ten credits in that genre. She had a reputation for being rather difficult to work with on the set, perhaps resulting in very few good movie roles after 1955. Still, Gloria Grahame is a star who is definitely worth remembering.

Biography

Gloria Grahame was born Gloria Hallward on November 28, 1923 in Los Angeles, California. Gloria was an acting pupil of her mother (stage actress and teacher Jean Grahame), and acted professionally while still in high school. In 1944 at age 19, MGM studio head Louis B. Mayer saw her on Broadway and gave her an MGM contract under the name Gloria Grahame, her mother's maiden name. Gloria's film debut in the title role of *Blonde Fever* (1944) was noteworthy (she was a waitress at the restaurant owned by Philip Dorn, who had the hots for her), but her first public recognition came on loan-out in 1946 in *It's a Wonderful Life* as Violet, the girl who all the guys in town except James Stewart had a crush on. Though her talent and sex appeal were of star quality, she did not fit the star pattern at MGM[106], who sold her contract to RKO in 1947. Here the same problem resurfaced; her best film in these years was made on loan-out, *In a Lonely Place* (1950), where she co-starred with Humphrey Bogart. Soon after, she left RKO. The 1950s, her best period, brought Gloria a Best Supporting Actress Oscar plus another Oscar nomination and typecast her as shady, inimitably sultry ladies in seven well-known film-noir classics.

Rumors of being difficult to work with on the set of *Oklahoma!* (1955) sidelined her film career from 1956 onward. She also suffered from marital and child-custody troubles. Eight years after her divorce from director Nicholas Ray, who was 12 years her senior (and reportedly had discovered her in bed with his 13 year old son), and after a subsequent marriage to Cy Howard ended in divorce, in 1960 she married her former stepson Anthony Ray who was almost 14 years younger than her. This led Nicholas Ray and Cy Howard to each sue for custody of each one's child by Grahame, delighting gossip columnists to no end, I am sure.

In 1960 Gloria resumed stage acting, combined with TV work and, from 1970, some mostly inferior films. Gloria was described by all as a serious, skillful actress; spontaneous, honest, and strong-willed; imaginative and curious; incredibly sexy but insecure about her looks[107] (prompting plastic surgery on her famous lips); loving

---

106 She probably did not appear wholesome looking enough for MGM.

107 I am not sure why; she always looked great to me!

appreciative male company; and "a bit loony." Her busiest period of British and American stage work ended abruptly in 1981 when she collapsed from cancer symptoms during a rehearsal. She returned to New York a few hours before she succumbed on October 5, 1981 at age 57 of stomach cancer and peritonitis

The 2017 movie *Film Stars Don't Die in Liverpool*, starring Annette Bening, is about the latter stages in the life of Gloria Grahame. Bening plays Grahame.

Awards

Grahame won a Best Supporting Actress award in 1953 for her performance in *The Bad and the Beautiful*. She was also nominated for a Best Supporting Actress in 1948 for her performance in *Crossfire*. And she was nominated for a Golden Globe award in 1953, again for her performance in *The Bad and the Beautiful*.

My Favorite Gloria Grahame Films

All of these films were from her best period of work - 1946 through 1955. As usual, I have included a couple of films that were apart from her best genre - film noir. They include:

1. *The Bad and the Beautiful* - 1952
2. *In a Lonely Place* - 1950
3. *The Big Heat* - 1953
4. *Crossfire* - 1947
5. *It's a Wonderful Life* - 1946
6. *The Greatest Show on Earth* - 1952
7. *Oklahoma* - 1955

1. *The Bad and The Beautiful* - 1952

Told in flashback form, the film traces the rise and fall of a tough, ambitious Hollywood producer, Jonathan Shields (Kirk Douglas), as seen through the eyes of various acquaintances, including a writer -James Lee Bartlow (Dick Powell), a star - Georgia Lorrison (Lana Turner), and a director - Fred Amiel (Barry Sullivan). Shields is a hard-driving, ambitious man who ruthlessly uses everyone - including the writer, star and director - on the way to becoming one of Hollywood's top movie makers.

In the flashback with Gloria Grahame, James Lee Bartlow (Dick Powell) is a contented professor at a small college who has written a bestselling book for which Shields has purchased the film adaptation rights. Shields wants Bartlow himself to write the film's script. Bartlow is not interested, but his shallow Southern belle wife, Rosemary (Gloria Grahame) is, so he agrees to do it for her sake. They go to Hollywood, where Shields is annoyed to find that her constant distractions are keeping her husband from his work. Shields gets his suave actor friend Victor "Gaucho" Ribera (Gilbert Roland) to keep her "occupied." Freed from interruption, Bartlow is able to make excellent progress on the script. Rosemary, however, runs off with Gaucho, and they are killed in a plane crash.

When the script is completed, Shields has the distraught Bartlow remain in Hollywood to help with the production as Shields takes over directing duties himself. A first-time director, Shields botches the job, which leads to his bankruptcy. Then Shields lets slip a casual remark that reveals his complicity in Rosemary's affair with Gaucho, so Bartlow walks out on him. Now able to view his late wife more objectively, Bartlow goes on to write a novel based upon his relationship with his deceased wife (something Shields had previously encouraged him to do) and wins a Pulitzer Prize for it.

> At 9 minutes and 32 seconds, Gloria Grahame's performance in this movie became the shortest to ever win an Oscar up to that time. Obviously, she was excellent in those 9 minutes and 32 seconds.

2. *In a Lonely Place* - 1950

Screenwriter Dixon Steele (Humphrey Bogart) has not had a hit screenplay "since the end of World War II," according to him. Faced with the odious task of scripting a trashy bestseller, he has hatcheck girl Mildred Atkinson - who is reading the novel - tell him the story in her own words back at his apartment. Later that night, Mildred is murdered and Steele is a prime suspect, according to the police inspector (Frank Lovejoy). His record of belligerence when angry and his macabre sense of humor work against him. Fortunately, lovely neighbor Laurel Gray (Gloria Grahame) gives him an alibi. Laurel proves to be just what Steele needs, and their friendship ripens into love. But she starts having doubts when he behaves erratically and also violently towards others - including being a perpetrator of what we might call "road rage" today. Will suspicion, doubt, and Steele's inner demons come between them?

Interestingly, *In a Lonely Rage* is directed by Grahame's soon-to-be ex-husband, Nicholas Ray. This brilliant film noir contains some of the best work of its three principals - Bogart, Grahame, and Ray. In fact, Bogart revealed that he felt it might have been his best performance. There is a lot of eerie feeling about Dixon Steele's character throughout the film - did he kill the hatcheck girl or not? And the truth is not revealed until the last scene of the film.

3. *The Big Heat* - 1953

Another crime drama/film noir starring Gloria Grahame and one of my favorite male movie stars, Glenn Ford. *The Big Heat* is sort of a crime film version of *High Noon* - one good man against the odds.

Dave Bannion (Glenn Ford) is a straight-laced cop on the trail of a vicious gang he suspects holds power over the police force. Bannion is tipped off after a colleague's suicide, and his fellow officers' suspicious silence lead him to believe that they are on the gangsters' payroll. When a bomb meant for him kills his wife instead, Bannion becomes a furious force of vengeance and justice, aided along the way by the gangster Vince Stone's (a brutal Lee Marvin) spurned girlfriend Debby Marsh (Gloria Grahame.) As Bannion and Debby fall further and further into the Gangland's insidious and brutal trap, they must use any means necessary (including murder) to get to the truth.

In a film directed by Fritz Lang, the three leads - Ford, Grahame, and Marvin - are all very good. Lang got the best out of Ford as a man against the world of crime and police corruption, but the most famous scene in the movie is when the brutally violent Vince Stone throws a pot of boiling coffee in the face of girlfriend Debby, scaring her for life. You can bet that after that incident, she was much more willing to help Ford than she was previously.

You can see why Gloria Grahame was more willing to help Glenn Ford after getting a pot of boiling coffee tossed in her face by Lee Marvin.

4. *Crossfire* - 1947

In spite of the presence of three well-known leading men named Robert - Robert Young, Robert Mitchum, and Robert Ryan - Gloria Grahame held her own in this outstanding crime drama.

A landmark Hollywood drama for its sharp look at the touchy subject of anti-Semitic attitudes in the U.S., *Crossfire* is set in a hotel just after the end of WW II and begins with the murder of a Jewish guest (Sam Levene). Homicide Capt. Finlay (Robert Young) finds evidence that one or more of a group of demobilized soldiers is involved in the death of the guest. In flashbacks, we see the night's events from different viewpoints as army Sgt. Keeley (Robert Mitchum) investigates on his own, trying to clear one of the men to whom circumstantial evidence points. Then the real, ugly motive for the killing begins to dawn on both Finlay and Keeley - anti-Semitism.

Gloria Grahame has a key role as a possible witness to the crime. Another film dealing with anti-Semitism was released the same year and won the Oscar for Best Picture. That film was *Gentleman's Agreement*, with Gregory Peck, Dorothy McGuire, and John Garfield.

Crossfire was nominated for five Academy Awards, including Robert Ryan for Best Supporting Actor and Gloria Grahame as Best Supporting Actress. A very good film with a plot involving a hate crime that continues to this day.

The Three Roberts - Mitchum, Ryan, and Young. One of them might be a murderer.

5. *It's a Wonderful Life* - 1946

We move away from crime dramas and over to one of America's all-time favorite movies - *It's a Wonderful Life*.

George Bailey (James Stewart), who always wanted to be an engineer, has instead spent his entire life giving of himself to the people of Bedford Falls. He has always longed to travel but never had the opportunity; instead, he is talked into taking over the Bailey Building and Loan after his father dies, in order to prevent rich skinflint Mr. Potter (Lionel Barrymore in a mean but good role) from taking over the entire town. All that prevents him from doing so is the building and loan. But on Christmas Eve, George's Uncle Billy (Thomas Mitchell) loses the business's $8,000 while intending to deposit it in the bank. Potter finds the misplaced money and hides it from Billy. When the bank examiner discovers the shortage later that night, George realizes that he will be held responsible and sent to jail and the company will collapse, finally allowing Potter to take over the town.

Thinking that his wife (Donna Reed), their young children, and others he loves will be better off with him dead because of his insurance money, he contemplates suicide. But the prayers of his loved ones result in a gentle angel named Clarence (Henry Travers) coming to earth to help George, with the promise of earning his wings. First he has to convince George, who now believes that it would have been better if he were never even born, that that idea is simply not the case. Gloria Grahame plays Violet Bick, the good looking girl that every boy in town covets except for James Stewart.

Despite initially performing poorly at the box office because of stiff competition at the time of its release, the film has become regarded as a classic and is a staple of Christmas television around the world. And it is probably the film that launched Gloria Grahame's career.

Gloria Grahame, with blond hair and frilly hat, among a group that includes James Stewart, Donna Reed, Ward Bond, H.B. Warner, Beulah Bondi, Frank Faylen, and Thomas Mitchell in the final scene from *It's a Wonderful Life.*

6. *The Greatest Show on Earth* - 1952

Despite a cast that included Gloria Grahame, Charlton Heston, Betty Hutton, James Stewart, Cornel Wilde, and Dorothy Lamour, and despite winning the Oscar for Best Picture, some have called *The Greatest Show on Earth* the worst film to ever win the Academy Award for Best Picture. While I personally like the film a lot, I have to agree that two of the movies that it beat - *High Noon* and *The Quiet Man* - were much better films.

The greatest show on earth is, of course, the circus, and this film is DeMille's tribune to that form of American entertainment[108]. To ensure a full profitable season, circus manager Brad Braden (Charlton Heston) engages The Great Sebastian (Cornel Wilde), though this moves his girlfriend Holly (Betty Hutton) from her hard-won center trapeze spot. Holly and Sebastian begin a dangerous one-upmanship duel in the ring, while he pursues her on the ground. Sebastian's former partner Angel (Gloria Grahame) is miffed by being kicked off her aerial act and instead forced to work with the elephants. Subplots involve the secret past of Buttons the Clown (James Stewart) and a major circus train crash, where heroic actions emerge. During the emergency rescue, we find out why Buttons always wears makeup.

With an outstanding cast and lots of suspense, intrigue, and action, *The Greatest Show on Earth* is still worth watching.

> Gloria Grahame almost did not get the part of Angel. Lucille Ball was scheduled to play the part, but found out she was pregnant and dropped out before filming began. That really does not sound like Lucy's forte anyway.

7. *Oklahoma!* - 1955

The film adaptation of the great Rodgers and Hammerstein Broadway hit is also a great movie.

---

108 The circus was a huge form of entertainment in the 1950s, when I was a kid. Not so much any more.

The story covers the Oklahoma territory just after the turn of the twentieth century as it approaches statehood.[109] Two young cowboys vie with a violent ranch hand and a traveling peddler for the hearts of the women they love. Curly McLain (Gordon MacRae) and Laurey Williams (Shirley Jones) carry on an on-again/off-again romance, while suspicious ranch hand Jud Fry (Rod Steiger) is waiting in the wings for Laurey's affections. At the same time, the fetching and somewhat promiscuous Ado Annie Carnes (Gloria Grahame in a very good performance) is trying to decide between her true love, Will Parker (Gene Nelson, who can sing and really dance) and the Persian salesman Ali Hakim (believe it or not, Eddie Albert!). There is a subplot about ranchers versus farmers, which we see in many westerns such as *Shane*, but this one is handled in a more lighthearted manner.

The supporting cast includes Charlotte Greenwood as Aunt Eller, the beautiful Barbara Lawrence as Gertie Cummings (she also has her eyes on Ali Hakim), Jay C. Flippen as the spokesman for the ranchers, and James Whitmore as the head of the farmers (and also Ado Annie's father). There is a nice blend of music, dancing, comedy, and also drama, especially surrounding the ranch hand. *Oklahoma!* won Oscars for Best Sound and Best Musical Scoring - no surprise there - and was nominated for two others. The film also includes a nice ballet sequence between dancers representing Curly, Laurey, and Jud.

Gloria Grahame's Ado Annie is an interesting study. Her character was supposed to provide mostly comic relief, but Grahame wanted to put a more sexy tone to her character, which she did. Also, since Grahame was tone deaf, but sung her own songs without dubbing, it required quite a bit of editing by the sound staff. She also appears only briefly in the musical numbers, because she was not much of a dancer at all; for example, in "The Farmer and the Cowman," she comes in and out to sing her lines. And in the title song, she appears now and then but avoids the parts where dancing is taking place. In spite of that, she was very effective in the part.

Oklahoma! was the first of a flurry of Rodgers and Hammerstein musicals that were brought to the big screen. After that, we got *Carousel* in 1956, *The King and I* also in 1956, *South Pacific* in 1958, *Flower Drum Song* in 1961, and the big one, *The Sound of Music*, in 1965.

---

109 Oklahoma officially became a state on November 16, 1907.

Eddie Albert, Gloria Grahame, and Gene Nelson in *Oklahoma!*

Gloria Grahame was a beautiful and alluring movie star whose best years were between 1946 to 1955. She was also a good actress, who won one Oscar and was nominated for one other. Grahame seemed to specialize in film noir, but was good in other dramas as well as comedies and musicals. Because of marital and child custody battles as well as a scandalous affair with her 13-year-old stepson, her career was never quite the same after the mid 1950s. Still, watching Gloria Grahame in her prime was something special.

20. Fredric March (1897-1975)

Let me say at the outset that I was never that big a fan of Fredric March. Like some actors who made their debut in silent films, he always seemed to be overacting to me. On the other hand, his two Best Actor Oscars and five overall Best Actor nominations are in and of themselves a reason to highlight him as a Forgotten Star. Although starting in banking, he turned to acting in 1920 and for the next 50+ years was a fixture in films, stage, and even television.

Biography

Born on Aug. 31, 1897, in Racine, Wis., and originally named Frederick McIntyre Bickel, Fredric March was the son of a small-time manufacturer, John F. Bickel, and the former Cora Brown Marcher. He worked as a bank teller during high school vacations and studied economics at the University of Wisconsin. An outstanding debater in college, March also played leading roles on the university stage. But when he came to New York in 1919 after a year in the Army, it was not to be an actor but a banker.

Shortly after his arrival, March had an appendicitis attack and after an appendectomy, he applied for a leave of absence from his trainee job at the National City Bank. and decided to pursue acting in the theater during that period. His professional debut, in 1920, came in Baltimore in "Deburau," in which he was also seen on Broadway for the first time. Then he dropped a couple of letters from his first name and adopted the first syllable of his mother's maiden name to come up, with the stage name of Fredric March. Versatile, cooperative, and eager, he was seldom without work.

In Denver in the summer of 1926, March joined a stock company whose leading lady was Florence Eldridge. While appearing together in Molnar's "The Swan," they fell in love, and were married in 1927 in Mexico. Their union, both personally and professionally, was to last for the rest of March's life.

In the late nineteen-twenties, Hollywood was struck by a crisis with the advent of sound in movies—many of the male stars of the silent movie era, such as John Gilbert, possessed voices that would not work in sound films. Gilbert's was squeaky high and effeminate. March struck Hollywood as the answer to a prayer; not only was he good looking, but also he had a rich, well-trained stage actor's voice.

His movie career began in 1929 with a featured role in *The Dummy*. He was an instant success, and soon some of the top female stars were clamoring to have him in their pictures. In the nineteen-thirties March appeared opposite Clara Bow, Ruth Chatterton, Claudette Colbert, Miriam Hopkins and finally Greta Garbo in *Anna Karenina*. Usually he was seen in romantic comedy or adventure roles, but in 1932 he switched to the serious dual role in *Dr. Jekyll and Mr. Hyde* and won his first Oscar.

March also occasionally returned to New York to appear onstage - opposite his wife in "Your Obedient Husband," a 1938 vehicle based on Samuel Pepys's diary. Unfortunately, it failed miserably. But March had more success in "The American Way" the following year, and from then on March was to deftly balance his work between movies and plays. "It has been my experience," he said years later, "that work on the screen clarifies stage portrayals and vice versa. You learn to make your face express more in making movies, and in working for the theater you have a sense of greater freedom."

In 1960, when the Marches appeared as William Jennings Bryan and his wife in the movie version of *Inherit the Wind*, about the Scopes "monkey trial," March learned the whole script, theater-style, in advance, before rehearsals. And although he was still a man of imposing good looks, he quite willingly submitted to make-up that made him bald.

His memorable screen performances included Noel Coward's *Design for Living*, in which he played a flip sophisticate; as the poet Robert Browning in *The Barretts of Wimpole Street*; as the alcoholic and suicidal actor opposite Janet Gaynor in *A Star Is Born*; and, of course, as the war-weary veteran in *The Best Years of Our Lives*, for which he won his second Best Actor Oscar.

In his Hollywood heyday, March felt he was becoming type-cast as a "costume actor" and vowed that once his long-term contracts had run out, he would never sign another multiple-picture deal. That was in the nineteen-forties. He was also intensely selective about the Broadway roles he would consider.

In 1949 March turned down the role of Willy Loman in the stage play "Death of a Salesman," which instead went to Lee J. Cobb. His reason was the following: "I didn't have the time to read it properly. Boy, I sure blew that one." The producers of the movie version of the play gave March his second chance, and he won another Oscar nomination in 1951 for his film portrayal of Willy Loman.

In 1940 March was one of many Hollywood personalities who ran afoul of Representative Martin Dies, then chairman of the House Committee on Un-American Activities, who had started a widely publicized hunt for Communists in the film-making community. In response, March openly defended the film community as patriotic, which eventually caused Dies to put him on a list of "politically clean" figures that included James Cagney, Humphrey Bogart, and the writer Philip Dunne.

In his later years, the Marches lived quietly, maintaining an apartment in New York and a 40-acre farm near New Milford, Connecticut. But age and ill health started to slow him down. He underwent prostate surgery for the second time while filming *The Iceman Cometh* in 1973. By then, the debilities of age had forced him to walk with the aid of a cane. Fredric March passed away from prostate cancer on April 14, 1975 at the age of 77.

Awards

Fredric March won two Oscars for Best Actor: in 1932, for *Dr. Jekyll and Mr. Hyde* and in 1947 for *The Best Years of Our Lives*. He was also nominated but did not win three other times:

- 1931 for *The Royal Family of Broadway*
- 1938 for *A Star Is Born*
- 1952 for *Death of a Salesman*

He also won one Golden Globe Award for Best Actor in a Drama, for *Death of a Salesman* in 1951 and was nominated for two others: 1960 for *Middle of the Night* and in 1965 for *Seven Days in May*.

March was nominated for three Best Actor Emmy awards but did not win: in 1955 for *The Best of Broadway* and for *Shower of Stars* and in 1957 for *Producers' Showcase*. He was also a nominee for three British BAFTA awards but did not win, including *Death of a Salesman* in 1953 and *Inherit the Wind* in 1961.

My Favorite Fredric March Films

I have to admit that I have never seen a couple of his best films from this era, including *A Star Is Born*, so I will just include the ones I am familiar with. For another good Fredric March film from the 1960's, check out *Seven Days in May*, with Burt Lancaster and Kirk Douglas. March is the U.S. President, Lancaster is outstanding as a general who thinks the President is a weakling and wants to take over the government, and Douglas as an officer who exposes the plot. March's speech to Lancaster as he confronts the traitorous general demonstrates he is anything but a weakling.

1. *The Best Years of Our Lives* - 1946
2. *Dr. Jekyll and Mr. Hyde* - 1931
3. *The Desperate Hours* - 1955
4. *Les Miserables* - 1935
5. *Death of a Salesman* - 1951
6. *Anthony Adverse* - 1936
7. *Inherit the Wind* - 1960

1. *The Best Years of Our Lives* - 1946

This is probably my single favorite movie, a beautiful story of the trials and tribulations of three veterans returning from World War II to their Midwest home of Boone City; this film is just as relevant today as it was 70+ years ago. Al Stephenson (Fredric March) is a banker who comes back to the bank and has the responsibility of approving loans for veterans who have no more collateral than military service but a desire to work hard. Homer Parrish (Harold Russell) had his hands blown off during the war and now must face a future with hooks instead of hands, wondering if he should break it off with his long-time girlfriend.[110] And Dana Andrews (Fred Derry) suffers from what they called "shellshock" in those days and what we now call post traumatic stress disorder (PTSD). The film follows their adjustment to civilian life as well as the women in their lives - Myrna Loy, Teresa Wright, Virginia Mayo, and Cathy O'Donnell. *The Best Years of Our Lives* is three hours long but takes its time to tell us the story of these men - their ups and their downs.

Fredric March has not seen his family in four years. His wife (Myrna Loy) has gotten used to him not being around, and he finds his two children (Teresa Wright and Michael Hall) have grown up while he was gone. Russell wants to break his wedding plans off with his girl friend

---

110 In real life, Harold Russell did lose his hands during the war, but it was during a training exercise accident rather than in combat. The effect, of course, is the same. William Wyler saw Russell in a training film and decided to cast him in this movie.

(Cathy O'Donnell) for her own good, while Andrews has a wife (Virginia Mayo) who does not care for him at all while, at the same time, he finds himself falling in love with Teresa Wright, and she with him, and they are perfect for each other.

The film is beautifully written, directed by William Wyler, and acted by all cast members. It swept the Oscars in 1947, winning seven, including Best Film but also six others:

- ➢ Best Actor (Fredric March)
- ➢ Best Supporting Actor (Harold Russell)[111]
- ➢ Best Director (William Wyler)
- ➢ Best Screenplay
- ➢ Best Editing
- ➢ Best Music

My only quibble with *The Best Years of Our Lives* is that Dana Andrews should have won Best Actor instead of Fredric March, and Andrews was not even nominated even though his role was tougher and required a wider range of emotions. But because Andrews tended to underplay his roles while March had a tendency to overact, March got the Oscar.

Dana Andrews, Fredric March, and Harold Russell flying home

2. *Dr. Jekyll and Mr. Hyde* - 1931

111 Harold Russell actually also won a special award, because the Academy did not think he was going to win for Best Supporting Actor.

This film was the first of Fredric March's two Oscar-winning performances, and it is easy to see why. The 1931 production is the first sound version of the Robert Louis Stevenson short story.

Good doctor Henry Jekyll (Fredric March) believes that there are two distinct sides to men - a good and an evil side. He believes that by separating the two sides, man can become liberated. He succeeds in his experiments with chemicals to accomplish this and transforms into Hyde to commit horrendous crimes. When he discontinues use of the drug it is already too late - Dr. Jekyll has already lost control to Mr. Hyde.

Because the Stevenson tale was only a short novel, to make it into a film, the director (Rouben Mamoulian) had to create extra subplots and additional characters. For example, in the book, Dr. Jekyll has no love interests, but in the film, he has a fiancée and also a barmaid that he has an affair with (as Hyde, of course). Also, in the novel, Hyde is rather handsome and devilish; in the movie, Hyde has a simian, ape-like look, so that it is classified as a horror film, which the book never was.

Fredric March as Mr. Hyde, rather ape-like in this version of the novel.

Fredric March won the 1931 Best Actor award, and why not? He basically played two completely different characters - Jekyll, who was inherently good, and Hyde, who was just as evil and more so. A good supporting cast included Miriam Hopkins as Ivy, the bar maid, Rose Hobart as Muriel Carew, his fiancée, and Holmes Hebert as Jekyll's friend, Dr. John Lanyon.

Until this time, Fredric March had only appeared in rather lightweight roles, but this film changed everything for him. And there have been scores of Jekyll and Hyde films made: perhaps the two other most famous ones were the 1920 silent film version starring John Barrymore, and the 1941 version with Spencer Tracy in the title role(s).

The remarkable Jekyll-to-Hyde transition scenes in this film were accomplished by manipulating a series of variously colored filters in front of the camera lens. Fredric March's Hyde makeup was in various colors, and the way his appearance registered on the film depended on which color filter was being shot through.

3. *The Desperate Hours* - 1955

This plot line has been used many times, but this is probably the best version of it: Convicts escaping from prison and breaking into a home and terrorizing the family members.

After escaping from prison, Glenn Griffin (Humphrey Bogart), his younger brother Hal (Dewey Martin) and a third inmate, Sam Kobish (Robert Middleton), randomly select a house in a well-to-do suburb of Indianapolis in which to hide out. The home belongs to the Hilliard family, Dan (Fredric March) and Ellie (Martha Scott), who live there with their 19-year old daughter Cindy (Mary Murphy) and their young son Ralph (child star Richard Eyer). They plan on staying only until midnight as Griffin is awaiting his girlfriend who will meet them with the money he had stashed away. When she doesn't arrive, however, their stay stretches out to several days. Dan Hilliard plays their game knowing that if he makes any attempt to contact the police, his family could be caught in the crossfire and killed. Of course, the authorities are conducting a statewide search for the escaped convicts and believe they must be holed up somewhere.

Another film directed by William Wyler, this one works well because of the pairing of the two stars - Bogart and March - who work well together. By the way, the exterior of the Hilliard home is the same exterior used in the television show *Leave it to Beaver*, which began two years later in 1957. The film co-stars Arthur Kennedy as the local police chief and Gig Young as Cindy Hilliard's boyfriend.

> In case you are wondering where you heard the name of Martha Scott before, she played Ben-Hur (Charlton Heston)'s mother in the 1959 Oscar winning epic, *Ben-Hur.*

Three escaped convicts - Humphrey Bogart, Dewey Martin, and Robert Middleton - terrorize Fredric March and Martha Scott in *The Desperate Hours.*

4. *Les Miserables* - 1935

This is likely the best sound, non-musical version of the Victor Hugo classic. In early 19th Century France an ex-convict, Jean Valjean

(Fredric March), who failed to report his to parole officer, is relentlessly pursued over a 20-year period by an obsessive policeman, Javert (Charles Laughton).

Ex-convict Jean Valjean (Fredric March), released from prison after 10 years serving in the galleys for stealing a loaf of bread to feed his sister's three starving children, is given 109 francs, a yellow passport, and sent out into a society that will have no part of him. While searching for food and a place to sleep, he chances upon a kindly bishop (Sir Cedric Hardwicke) who inspires him to 'give...not take.' Valjean steals a pair of candlesticks from the church, but when he is arrested by the police, the bishop says that he gave the candlesticks to Valjean, and that they were not stolen.

Inspired by the bishop's kindness, Valjean decides to break his parole and create a new life, raising himself from unwanted convict to mayor of Montreuil, distinguished by his charitable works, e.g., his attempts to re-unite the dying Fantine Lesrolles (Florence Eldridge) with her young daughter Cosette (Marilyn Knowlden and later Rochelle Hudson as the adult Cosette). Unfortunately, police inspector Emil Javert (Charles Laughton) learns of his whereabouts and vows to relentlessly track him down for his parole violation and return him to the galleys for the rest of his life.

Fredric March is very good as Jean Valjean, but Charles Laughton is even better as the persistent, ruthless Javert, who will stop at nothing to bring down Jean Valjean. Florence Eldridge, March's wife in real life[112], is the doomed Fantine, and Rochelle Hudson plays the grownup Cosette. The film was nominated for four Oscars, including Best Picture, but did not win any; in fact, it lost out to *Mutiny on the Bounty*, another Charles Laughton vehicle.

This was the last film made by 20th Century Pictures before it merged with Fox Film Corporation to form 20th Century Fox. And interestingly, when the director realized that some of the extras were chewing gum in their scenes, several of the scenes had to be reshot. (I guess there wasn't a lot of gum in 19th century France.)

---

112 They were married for almost 50 years until his death in 1975.

5. *Death of a Salesman* - 1951

The first film adaptation of Arthur Miller's Pulitzer Prize-winning play, *Death of a Salesman* is brought to the screen by producer Stanley Kramer. The salesman of the title is Willy Loman (Fredric March), who has spent his entire life pursuing success, only to find himself a middle-aged failure. The shock of this realization causes Willy's mind to wander between the past and the present, as he muses on lost opportunities, shattered dreams, and his turbulent relationship with his oldest son, Biff (Kevin McCarthy). Willy ultimately loses all contact with reality, which results in fate's final blow.[113] Mildred Dunnock brilliantly recreated her stage role as Willy's long-suffering wife, Linda ("Attention! Attention must be paid to this man.").

The 1951 film - there was also a 1985 version with Dustin Hoffman as Willy Loman - had a darkness to it, and was very melancholy, depressing, desperate, and hopeless; as a result, it is an emotionally exhausting film to watch. *Death of a Salesman* does not leave you feeling good at the end but it is definitely worth watching.

Death of a Salesman was nominated for five Oscars but did not win any, including Fredric March for Best Actor, Kevin McCarthy for Best Supporting Actor, and Mildred Dunnock for Best Supporting Actress. It did win four Golden Globe awards, however, including March for Best Actor and McCarthy for Best Supporting Actor.

Kevin McCarthy (Biff Loman) was in a number of good films among his total of 206 movie and television credits; but the one he will always be remembered for is as Dr. Miles Bennell in the horror/science fiction classic from 1956, *Invasion of the Body Snatchers*, a really eerie film without one monster shown in the film. McCarthy died in 1910 at the age of 96.

---

113 Lee J. Cobb, who'd played Willy on Broadway, had been blacklisted by Hollywood because of his alleged "leftist" politics and thus was denied the opportunity to star in the film version. But Fredric March was just as good as his replacement.

A completely distraught Kevin McCarthy attempting to convince psychiatrist Whit Bissell that he is NOT crazy, in the 1956 classic *Invasion of the Body Snatchers.*

6. *Anthony Adverse* - 1936

A good 1936 adventure film/costume drama with Fredric March in the title role of an orphan with an "adverse" background who nevertheless strives to make his fortune.

In late 18th century Italy, a beautiful young woman (Anita Louise) finds herself married to a rich but cruel older man (a very nasty Claude Rains). However, she is in love with another, younger man, Denis Moore (Louis Hayward at the beginning of his career.) When the husband finds out, he kills Moore in a swordfight, and takes his wife on a long trip throughout Europe. Months later, she dies giving birth to a son. The husband leaves the child at a convent, where he is raised until the age of 10; then he is apprenticed to a local merchant (Edmund Gwenn), who gives him the name "Anthony Adverse" because of the adversity in his life. But his adversity has only begun. Anthony is in love with Angela (Olivia de Havilland), an aspiring opera singer, but he travels to Africa to recover his grandfather's fortune rather than stay with her. There he becomes involved in slave trading. When he returns from Cuba, Africa, and Paris, things have changed for Angela - and for him.

Anthony Adverse was awarded four Oscars, including Gale Sondergaard for Best Supporting Actress as the vile housekeeper,[114] and was nominated for three others, including Best Picture. At this time, it was the most expensive film ever made by Warner Brothers at over one million dollars, and was also 141 minutes long, a lengthy film in those days.

This would certainly not be the last time that Louis Hayward would be involved in a swordfight. In fact, he was in quite a number of swashbucklers, including one of my favorites, the 1939 hit, *The Man in the Iron Mask*. I count a total of seven others, including one called *The Lady in the Iron Mask*. Why not?

A dashing Louis Hayward with Joan Bennett in *The Man in the Iron Mask*, one of the best swashbucklers of all time.

7. *Inherit the Wind* - 1960

Based on a real-life case in 1925 - the Scopes monkey trial, two great lawyers argue the case for and against a science teacher accused of the crime of teaching evolution. Perhaps the best feature of *Inherit the Wind* is the matching of wits of the two lead actors and opposing attorneys -

---

114 This was the first year in which a Best Supporting Actress award for given by the Academy.

Spencer Tracy as Henry Drummond and Fredric March as Matthew Harrison Brady. Drummond is really Clarence Darrow while Brady is actually William Jennings Bryan.

In a small Southern town, a school teacher, Bertram Cates (Dick York), is about to stand trial. His offense: violating a state law by introducing to his students the concept that man descended from the lower life forms, a theory of the naturalist Charles Darwin - in other words, evolution. The town is excited because appearing for the prosecution will be Matthew Brady (Fredric March), a noted statesman and three-time presidential candidate. A staunch foe of evolution and a Biblical scholar, Brady will sit beside prosecuting attorney Tom Davenport (Elliott Reed), in the courtroom of Judge Coffey.

The teacher's defense is to be handled by the equally well-known Henry Drummond (Spencer Tracy), one of America's most controversial legal minds and a long-standing acquaintance and adversary of Brady. An influential newspaperman, E.K. Hornbeck (Gene Kelly, in a rare non-musical role)[115] of the *Baltimore Herald*, has persuaded Drummond to represent Cates, and ensured that his newspaper and a radio network will provide nationwide coverage of the case. As the trial progresses, Judge Coffey clearly favors Matthew Brady in almost every ruling and objection.

The best thing about this film is the outstanding work of the two stars, Tracy and March. Tracy was nominated for a Best Actor Oscar but lost out to Burt Lancaster in *Elmer Gantry*. A truly outstanding supporting cast includes Harry Morgan (Colonel Potter on *M.A.S.H.* as Judge Coffey, March's real-life wife, Florence Eldridge, as Brady's wife, plus Claude Akins, Elliott Reed, and Noah Berry, Jr. But it is really Tracy and March that make the film work.

---

115 Drummond is based on the real reporter and writer, H.L. Mencken.

Two greats - Spencer Tracy and Fredric March - on opposite sides in *Inherit the Wind*.

The more I think of it, the more I realize how good an actor Fredric March actually was. In film after film, regardless of the part, he displayed true talent and a real dedication to his craft. He deserves to be a "not forgotten" star.

ACKNOWLEDGEMENTS

My special thanks go out to two sources that make researching classic films a lot easier:

1. The International Movie Data Base, or IMDB
2. Wikipedia